Collecting
Movie
Memorabilia

Books by Sol Chaneles

The Movie Makers
The Open Prison
that pestilent cosmetic, rhetoric
Three Children of the Holocaust
Losing in Place
The New Civility
Santa Makes a Change

Collecting
Movie
Memorabilia

SOL CHANELES

Arco Publishing Company, Inc.
New York

Published by Arco Publishing Company, Inc.
219 Park Avenue South, New York, N.Y. 10003

Library of Congress Cataloging in Publication Data

Chaneles, Sol.
    Collecting movie memorabilia.

    Includes index.
    1. Moving-picture paraphernalia—Collectors and
collecting.   I.   Title.

PN1995.9.C54C5   791.43'075   76-44008
ISBN 0-668-04048-3 (Library Edition)

Printed in the United States of America

To YP

Contents

Introduction

Collecting movie memorabilia is a source of pleasure for more people each year. Its growing popularity is causing scarcity in the supply in many areas, especially posters, and with it rising prices. However, that makes the search—prospecting for memorabilia—all the more pleasurable.

This book is intended to help beginning collectors understand some aspects of the history of certain memorabilia and to be able to deal knowledgeably and realistically with the marketplace. I have also kept in mind the needs of those people who have accumulated movie-related materials over the years as a casual hobby and who would now like to become serious collectors. Although this book tells about several of the extraordinary discoveries and purchases made in recent years—some involving many thousands of dollars for a single item—I have tried to emphasize movie collectibles that are within the reach of many different collectors' budgets. There is, for example, a way of adding to a collection an antique automobile costing fifteen thousand dollars that belonged to a famous silent screen star, but there is little or no movie related interest in the car although it would appeal to antique car collectors. Although a few movie collectibles are very expensive—such as a "Camille" poster for under five thousand dollars and a handwritten, autograph letter of Marilyn Monroe for two thousand dollars—most movie memorabilia, at least until 1980, will be available for between a few dollars and a few hundred dollars.

Ordinarily, movie memorabilia do not require special care and are therefore easy to enjoy and to bring delight to others. Of course, they require care and protection when moving them about.

A few kinds of movie memorabilia collectibles have been omitted from the book. I have not included much information about films themselves, for example. One- and two-reel 16mm silent and sound films

9

originally made for home, school, or club showing are growing in popularity among collectors. However, a projector is needed to enjoy the films, and while there is a lively collector's market for the films (prices range from thirty-five dollars for a late "Popeye" two-reeler to over two hundred dollars for a French language "Donald Duck" two-reeler) it is still generally a special area for collectors and very little information is presently available. One of the main problems in providing information about collecting films is that since copies are easily made it is difficult and expensive to find out the quality of the film stock and the condition of the film at the time of purchase.

There is little or no discussion about such collectibles as personal clothing of the stars or the costumes they wore in famous movie scenes, and, again, this is mainly because there are too few collectors of these objects and information is not readily available for potential collectors. Perhaps in a future edition of this book it will be possible to present useful information about movie memorabilia that have been omitted here.

As a general rule, when trying to obtain specific memorabilia from a dealer who does not himself have the material you want but is confident that he can get it for you, be sure to get a price quotation in advance. Due to the fact that movie related materials are becoming scarcer each day, prices tend to climb upwards and a price quoted in advance is a good way to protect your collecting budget.

In writing this book I have actually prospected, bought, sold, and traded every category of movie memorabilia mentioned. I have a collection which I enjoy enormously and I have had many wonderful experiences and made many new friends in assembling it.

CHAPTER ONE

Black-and-White Movie Stills

Stills, those amazing 8″ x 10″ sheets of chemically treated paper, are going to remain the most popular collector's item of movie memorabilia for a long time. Stills are easy to store and display in a ring binder, carton, or metal filing cabinet; they can be attractively framed and mounted; you can have them blown up to poster size or reduced to postage stamp size. Carefully selected and protected against folds, tears, excessive moisture, or heat, stills will continue to increase in value and will remain by far the item most easily traded with other collectors. Prices of stills increase slowly, unlike those of other movie memorabilia, so that it is possible to build an important, very selective collection of originals that will be every bit as fresh, entertaining, and unforgettable as the movies they represent—as well as being increasingly valuable and profitable.

Collections of stills may be based on almost any criterion that pleases. I have seen fascinating, really quite remarkable collections of stills of movie scenes that never appeared in the movies. "Out-take" or "cut" collections of stills (there are also special collections of sound track out-takes) are popular among very competitive collectors who can then have both a rare collection and items that can be readily rented or sold to writers for magazines and television who are on the lookout for stories that are bound to delight. One beautiful and rare out-take is from the classic film "All Quiet on the Western Front." It shows Lew Ayres and Zazu Pitts in a very touching farewell scene. Zazu Pitts, however, does not appear in the final version of the movie. This rare photo, like many others in the long history of the movies, was taken during dress rehearsals or specially posed just seconds before the director called for a *take*. Publicity photographs simply had to be in the hands of the advertising and publicity agents for the studios *before* the movie was finished—sometimes three to six months before the final version of the

11

Mia Farrow in "Rosemary's Baby."

Deanna Durbin in "100 Men and a Girl."

GREAT BLACK AND WHITE STILLS

Collection: Sol Chaneles

Boris Karloff in "Before I Hang."

Thomas Meighan in "Manslaughter."

Wallace Beery and Jackie Cooper in "Treasure Island."

Joan Crawford and Jackie Coogan in "Old Clothes."

Humphrey Bogart and Peter Lorre in "The Maltese Falcon."

James Dean, Sal Mineo, and Natalie Wood in "Rebel Without a Cause."

film came from the editing rooms. By the time stills were on the desks of newspaper and magazine editors around the country and in the offices of the movie managers waiting to put them on display, some of the scenes shown in the stills had been edited out and were left on the cutting room floor.

Nearly every movie-goer remembers leaving a movie and taking a few moments to look at the stills in the lobby or on the walls on either side of the box office and saying about a particular scene: "But *that* wasn't in the movie!" This probably happened many times and many movie-goers made a game of checking the stills after seeing a movie to see how many of the scenes shown in the stills had actually been cut. Sometimes, a *cut* still is of the first or early bit part of a performer who went on to become a famous star. Such stills are often the only photographic record of the star's debut in the movies and they are precious objects, indeed.

Another exciting collection I've seen is based on extraordinary *stunt* scenes from the movies. Actors hurtling through the air as they fall off cliffs and rooftops, jumping out of flaming wrecks, or jumping into danger—these are phenomenally entertaining stills that take much patience to collect, but they show a side of the movies that made the movies what they are.

Another great collection is of *close-ups* as they appeared in the movies, not enlargements of a scene or a head and shoulders shot, but lovely, or moving, or richly emotional stills of the head of an actor or actress in a memorable moment. Such close-up stills are not found very often because publicity departments preferred to promote a movie on the basis of a full-length posed portrait of a personality or a scene from the movie. A close-up could mislead the prospective ticket buyer by conveying the wrong emotion.

I've also seen a very amusing and very valuable collection of stills showing errors made by the movie company. At some time, you have probably seen a movie in which at a particular moment a microphone appears from 'nowhere' or you have seen the shadow of a microphone on the back wall of a room. This is probably the most common technical error made by movie makers. There have been countless other errors that discerning collectors have identified and they have been able to prospect for stills that show the mistakes: such as an actress wearing a dress in a scene that follows a scene in which the dress was supposed to have been destroyed, or a scene from a period movie that included, by error, a view of all or a portion of some modern object, for instance, an electric light in a Biblical movie.

There are highly specialized collections showing movie villains or naval heroes and the like, but most collectors are interested in general collections, at least during their first few years of collecting. One of the most pleasing kinds of general movie still collections is of scenes from movies that show the lead player or players in the same scene with other principal members of the cast. A good name for this kind of collection would be the "studio company." All the major studios of the past maintained a company of featured players at great expense under long term contracts. These players, like the actors in a repertory company, played important character roles together in dozens and dozens, and sometimes hundreds, of movies in a lifetime before the camera. They were usually given movie credits as: "Also Starring," "Featuring," and "Also Featuring." It was their unforgettable faces, their incomparable voices, and their unique, immediately recognizable mannerisms in whatever part they played that immediately enhanced a movie's entertainment value. It would have been financially risky for a studio to launch new starring players without the backbone of the "studio company." And what a company of individuals who performed so brilliantly together! A movie without C. Aubrey Smith as the stern but loving patriarch just wasn't a movie. Sophisticated comedies that needed a cynical, always drunk newspaper reporter wouldn't work without Roscoe Kearns or Ned Sparks. What millions and millions of movie lovers around the world remember first about the movies are the great faces of the great studio company actors—the "Also Starring" greats from movie's Golden Age: Eugene Pallette, Hermione Baddeley, Charlotte Greenwood, Edna May Oliver, Gene Lockhart, Grant Mitchell, Otto Kruger, Mary Boland, Billie Burke, Akim Tamiroff, May Robson, Byron Foulger, Billy Gilbert, Allen Jenkins, Charles Starrett, Lee Tracy, Estelle Winwood, Chill Wills, Sara Haden, and Alan Hale, among at least two hundred other long-time members of studio companies. Millions of fans are now familiar with the studio company performers as a result of their movies being shown on television. So much of the style and memorable quality of the most popular movies of the 1970s—movies that were made during the 1930s and early 1940s—was produced by the lively, wonderful qualities of the studio companies. Their freshness and fine acting is preserved in a large number of collectible black-and-white stills.

GREAT SCENES OF
GREAT DIRECTORS

Collection: Sol Chaneles

Alexander Korda's "Henry VIII."

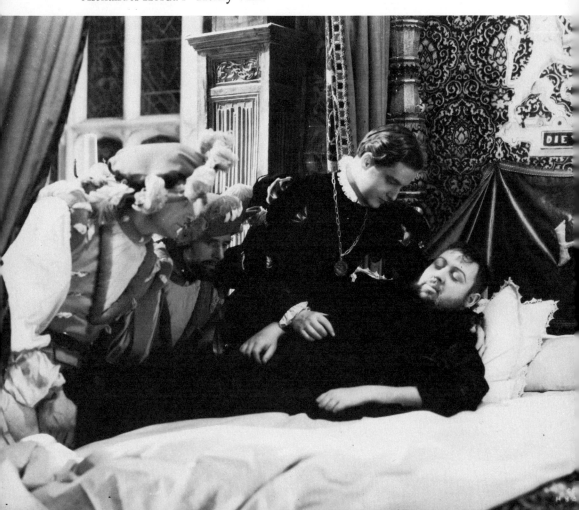

Cecil B. De Mille's "The Ten Commandments."

Alfred Hitchcock's "The Lady Vanishes."

D. W. Griffith's "Birth of a Nation."

Mel Brooks' "Blazing Saddles."

Victor Fleming's "The Wizard of Oz."

A RARE CUT SCENE

Zazu Pitts and Lew Ayres in a rare scene cut from "All Quiet on
the Western Front."

FABULOUS "A" WESTERNS

William S. Hart.

Hoot Gibson in
"Powdersmoke Range."

Collection:
Sol Chaneles

Randolph Scott in "Colt .45."

Alan Ladd in "The Big Land."

Robert Mitchum in "Hoppy Serves a Writ," which is of interest mainly because Robert Mitchum appears for the first time—as an extra.

Broderick Crawford in "When the Daltons Rode."

During the 1970s, when collecting stills made a giant leap in terms of the number of people who began collecting and in the increasing quality of the materials that they could choose from, many different kinds of interests developed. However, the kinds of stills which are in greatest demand among collectors and which are the basis for the most popular and reasonably priced collections are:

1. Laurel and Hardy, Marx Brothers, Ritz Brothers, and other comedy teams.
2. Horror films such as the "Frankenstein" series, "Dracula," and "The Invisible Man."
3. Detective and "private eye" mysteries such as "The Maltese Falcon," "The Thin Man," and "The Lady Vanishes."
4. Westerns and "B" Westerns, especially the "B" Westerns.
5. The weekly cliffhangers, usually twelve- to thirteen-week serials filled with adventure and thrills.
6. Science Fiction.
7. Individual stars: Humphrey Bogart, Marilyn Monroe, Judy Garland, Leslie Howard, Shirley Temple.
8. Directors' movies: John Ford, William Wyler, Ernst Lubitsch.
9. Musicals: "The Golddiggers," "An American in Paris," "Broadway Melody."
10. Political movies such as "Citizen Kane," "Mr. Smith Goes to Washington," and "The Last Hurrah."
11. Extraordinary movies such as "Horsefeathers," "Casablanca," "The Wizard of Oz," "The Dawn Patrol," and "The Informer."
12. Acting teams: Abbott and Costello, Jeannette MacDonald and Nelson Eddy, Ginger Rogers and Fred Astaire, Katherine Hepburn and Spencer Tracy.
13. The "Sex Symbols": Marlene Dietrich, Jean Harlow, Rita Hayworth.
14. Tarzan and other jungle movies.
15. The great fantasies such as "King Kong," "Topper," and "Snow White and the Seven Dwarfs."

There is no end to the number of entertaining and valuable collections that can be started. If you are interested in furniture, you will gain great pleasure by hunting down stills from period movies. The best and most elaborately detailed period movies were made with the assistance of scholars of the period, antique experts, and curators of museums. The exquisite movie, "Romeo and Juliet," (1938) was set in Renaissance Italy, around the middle of the fourteenth century. The artistic detail in the movie is fantastic. When original chairs and chests of the period could not be found in private homes or museums, the studio employed old-world craftsmen to make exact copies. Some of the pieces that were reconstructed are so meticulous in workmanship and so faithful to detail that they are as beautiful as the originals.

When the major studios began to shut down during the 1950s, special auctions and sales were run to dispose of the vast warehouses of furniture they had accumulated. Some of the prices paid for studio-made replicas of period furniture were as high and in many cases higher than those for less beautiful originals from the period which had been copied for the movie. For similar reasons, there are outstanding stills and the basis for novel and valuable memorabilia collections on sailing ships, automobiles, clocks, armor, steamboats, early trains of the West, European churches filmed on location, Roman chariots, military uniforms, prop paintings and statues, palace banquets, miniatures, courtrooms, prisons, and even unique shots of buildings that were demolished a long time ago.

The delight and worth of a collection does not depend on whether it is general or specialized. The variety, beauty, and condition of your collection will determine pleasure and worth. In short, quality is what you are likely to find appealing and what you should be trying to achieve. However, starting a collection of stills with a general interest in mind offers many advantages, chief of which is being able to see, feel, and experiment with the immense variety of stills of a more specialized character. In the long run, a first-rate general collection will be larger and considerably more valuable than a specialized collection. Although starting a general collection is not as demanding of time and expense as starting a specialized collection, you are bound to find, over a period of time, that it will become more demanding and probably will require more of an investment.

Many collectors of black-and-white stills who began collecting during the late 1960s and early 1970s started and stayed with specialized collections. Some are happy that they did so, while others would have liked to move in a more general direction but find that it is difficult to branch out. There are, however, some collectors who began with modest-sized specialized collections and who have been able to broaden their collections in a more general direction while continuing their special interests, especially after they have developed a certain reputation among collectors and dealers for the size and quality of their specialization. Among the more popular special collections that were developed in the early 1970s were: the James Bond "007" movies, Marie Dressler, James Dean, early Brando, Busby Berkeley musicals, Harold Lloyd, Humphrey Bogart, and James Cagney.

On hundreds of college campuses across the country, teachers and students have become avid collectors with special interests in the early work of certain directors and in the early social films of the 1930s. One of the most outstanding specialized collections, with 10,000 different stills, is of Lana Turner. There are many collectors with glamorous black-and-white stills of Joan Crawford's costumes, and it is getting more and more difficult to build a collection of Shirley Temple, the early Charles Boyer, or the earliest W.C. Fields. Each week hundreds of new collectors continue to find new specialized interests: movies based on Shakespeare's plays; movie animals such as Rin Tin Tin, Lassie, or Silver; pirate scenes; skiing; mining; ghosts; and vocalists who perform unusual dramatic roles.

One reasonable way to start a collection of black-and-white stills is to choose a phase of movie history: the early silents—before 1925; the major, feature-length silents—1925-1930; the early talkies—1930-1933; the Thirties; the Forties; the Fifties; or the Sixties. The first year or so of collecting can be used to become familiar with the wide range of materials produced during the various phases and within a particular phase. Once a phase has been chosen, the collector can begin to cultivate more specialized interests such as styles of comedy, particular actors and actresses, or the work of a particular production studio or director.

One of the most popular ways to start a collection is to concentrate on some aspect of movies that have won Academy Awards. Stills from Award-winning pictures do not tend to increase in value as do most other stills. This is because an Award winner is often re-released, along with a good deal of advertising and publicity, so that the market is filled with overly familiar 8″ x 10″s.

Whether general or specialized, the real quality of a collection will depend on the care given to building the collection and the pleasure it expresses. In 1974, a young woman of eighteen who was about to go off to college decided to dispose of her collection of stills of zoo animals she had seen in movies from the time she was ten. She had carefully and lovingly collected and preserved over a thousand stills. People thought she would be disappointed when she offered her collection for sale to a local museum. Most of those people were delightfully shocked when the young collector was paid $5000 for her stills.

One important advantage in starting a collection with specialized interests is that you will learn what the strengths of memorabilia dealers and dealer-collectors are very quickly. Once a specialized collection is started it is easy enough to appreciate the extent and quality of similar specialized collections. Another advantage of the specialized collection is that it permits keeping a closer watch on the changing values in similar areas of specialization. For example, the value of a collection of stills about sky adventures in the early mono-planes or bi-planes will be about the same, whether the movie was made in 1930 with the great movie air hero of the time, Richard Barthelmess, or in 1940 as a Saturday serial with performers whose names never appeared in the title cards. A change in value of one is likely to be reflected in a similar change in value of the other.

One of the most rapidly growing areas for collectors is the Saturday serial. Whatever the movie style: sky or jungle adventure, spy, detective or evil genius cliffhanger, race, chase, or history, the serials were always based on feature films that were popular in the late 1920s or early 1930s and costs tend to be about the same.

During the 1930s and 1940s, many movie-goers made up their minds to buy a ticket for a particular show only after looking at the stills mounted in windowed panels along the outside walls of the theater. It didn't take long to find out what kind of movie it *really* was because a picture, as the Chinese say, is worth a thousand words. Whether you could expect spine-chilling goose-bumps, a good cry, the best laugh in a long time, or simple dramatic distraction could be "told" in the twinkling of an eye. If you could say: "This is my kind of movie!" you paid the price and went in. The very best black-and-white stills can still tell you right away whether it would have been your kind of movie. This is because studio publicity photographers went to great lengths to pose the subjects in the most effective way, arranging the lighting, capturing just the right mood, making certain of each detail. As a result, the posed still of an action scene will always enjoy greater value than either the blow-up made from discarded film footage or the portrait.

Portraits are limited but nonetheless affecting, pleasure-giving mementos. They were used by movie studios exclusively for advertising in news-

FABULOUS "B" WESTERNS

Roy Rogers.

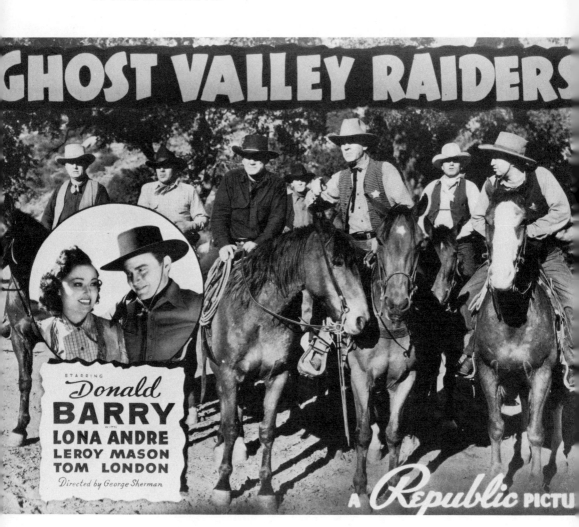

GHOST VALLEY RAIDERS

STARRING
Donald
BARRY
WITH
LONA ANDRE
LEROY MASON
TOM LONDON
Directed by George Sherman

A *Republic* PICTU

Donald Barry.

Johnny Mack Brown.

CHARLES **STARRETT** in **COWBOY IN THE CLOUDS**

DUB TAYLOR · JULIE DUNCAN
and THE JESTERS
with Jimmy Wakely and his Saddle Pals
STORY AND SCREEN PLAY BY ELIZABETH BEECHER
Directed by BENJAMIN KLINE A COLUMBIA PICTURE

BAD MEDICINE FOR BAD MEN..AS HE WRITES THE LAW IN RED-HOT L

BUCK **JONES** in
"THE EAR AT THE WINDOW"

Chapter 11
of the thrill-thundering chapter-play
"WHITE EAGLE"

with
RAYMOND HATTON · DOROTHY FAY
Screen play by Arch Heath, Morgan B. Cox, John Cutting, Lawrence E. Taylor

Charles Starrett.

"Lash" La Rue.

Buck Jones.

papers and magazines. Most were posed to be flattering or glamorous, and only in rare and outstanding cases were they intended to express the memorable qualities of a star or character actor. Because of their stiffness, portrait stills were never used near the box office. The main value of portrait stills (and there are thousands of enthusiastic collectors with specialized portrait interests) is in their being a record of a performer at a particular moment in a career. No collection could be complete without a number of portrait stills.

With only a few rare exceptions, black-and-white movie stills are 8″ x 10″ in size. Rarities are the 4″ x 6″ photographs printed in that size and not reduced or cropped to that size, and the less rare 5″ x 8″s, also originally printed in that size. For original photos of first release movies, the surface finish of stills is nearly always a high gloss. Stills from the late 1920s and early 1930s are in a semi-gloss and sometimes a matte (dull) finish. Before 1925, all stills were made with a matte finish and the color was as often the brownish sepia that photographers and the public were fond of at the time. It should be kept in mind that a high-gloss still from the period before 1925 is probably a recently made copy.

Even the best preserved glossy stills, like certain types of glazed vases, will, if they are originals, show some minor crackling in the glossy finish. The gloss finish on photographs is produced on the surface of the paper by a process of very slow heating after prolonged immersion in cold water. In time, impurities in the air and changes in humidity cause crackling in the gloss, and this is the only way to be certain that the still is an original made for a first release movie. Duplicates, or "dupes" as they are called, are generally less valuable than originals—even when well made. "Dupes" of "dupes" should be avoided since they tend to be very inferior copies. As a rule, a "dupe" costs half the price of a good quality original.

How old a still is is not always a good indication of its value. The following are average prices (as of 1976) for black-and-white 8″ x 10″ stills, in mint to good condition, originals only.

Action Scenes or Portraits

Year	Actor or Actress	Price
Before 1915	Pearl White	$ 25.00
	Charles Chase	15.00

	Tom Mix	35.00
	Dustin Farnum	50.00
1915–1919	Fatty Arbuckle	40.00
	Douglas Fairbanks	25.00
	Theda Bara	15.00
	Lon Chaney, Sr.	50.00
	Mary Pickford	20.00
1920–1925	Laurel & Hardy	100.00
	Emil Jannings	75.00
	Warner Oland	35.00
	Harold Lloyd	60.00
1925–1929	Lew Ayres	15.00
	Bela Lugosi	100.00
	Lawrence Olivier	25.00
1930–1935	Clark Gable	50.00
	W. C. Fields	25.00
	Victor McGlaglen	15.00
	Mae West	35.00
1936–1939	Pat O'Brien	10.00
	Louise Rainer	20.00
	Gary Cooper	25.00
	Mickey Rooney	10.00
	Judy Garland	20.00

From 1940 on, most stills can be bought for five to ten dollars, on the average.

Movies

Title	*Price*
Adventures of Huckleberry Finn	$ 7.50
Alexander Graham Bell	10.00
Alice's Restaurant	8.50
An American In Paris	12.50
Andy Hardy Gets Spring Fever	9.00
The Bad Seed	12.00
Barbarella	10.00
Becky Sharp	20.00
Ben Hur	15.00
The Birdman of Alcatraz	5.00

A Connecticut Yankee in King Arthur's Court	10.00
Cry Havoc	12.50
Curse of Frankenstein	15.00
David Copperfield	5.00
Destry Rides Again	9.50
Dick Tracy	10.00
Dr. No	12.50
East of Eden	15.00
Evel Knievel	5.00
The Four Horsemen of the Apocalypse	35.00
Funny Girl	5.00
The Glass Menagerie	7.50
Guadalcanal Diary	8.50
A Hard Day's Night	10.50
A Hole in the Head	5.00
I Am a Fugitive from a Chain Gang	15.00
Ice Follies of 1939	12.50
The Jazz Singer	22.50
Kind Hearts and Coronets	6.50
La Dolce Vita	7.50
Lady Be Good	7.50
Little Caesar	10.00
The Mark of Zorro	12.50
Midnight Cowboy	5.00
The Misfits	15.00
Peck's Bad Boy	20.00
The Prisoner of Zenda	16.00
The Red Shoes	8.00
The Return of Mr. Moto	7.50
Sayonara	7.50
Show Boat	8.50
Stage Door	8.00
Tarzan Escapes	9.00
The Third Man	6.50
Under Two Flags	12.00
Walk a Crooked Mile	6.50
The Wizard of Oz	10.00
Young Mr. Lincoln	5.00

SOME GREAT COMICS

Charlie Chaplin.

Collection: Sol Chaneles

Woody Allen in "Take the Money and Run."

Harold Lloyd in "Harold Lloyd's World of Comedy."

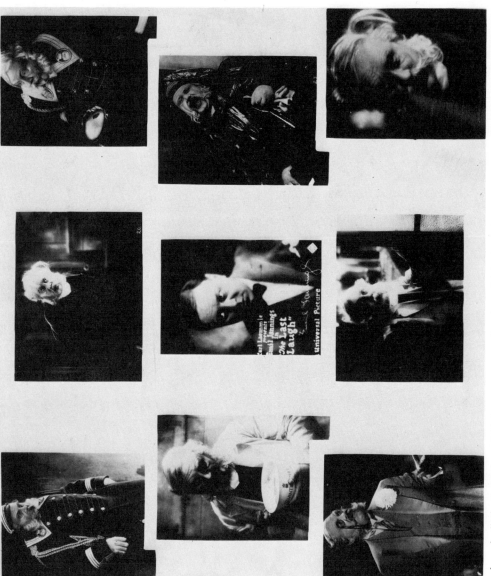

Emil Jannings in "The Last Laugh." A rare, unusual series of black-and-white photographs on a single 8" x 10" sheet with captions on the reverse.

CARL LAEMMLE *presents*

"EMIL JANNINGS"
IN

"THE LAST LAUGH"

A U. F. A. Production

At a Glance

Title.........."THE LAST LAUGH"
Brand..........U. F. A. Production, Released Through
    UNIVERSAL.
Star...........EMIL JANNINGS.
Director.......F. W. MURNAU.
Author........CARL MAYER.
Cameraman....Carl Freund.
Technique Experts..Hertl & Rohrich.
Time..........Present.
Local..........Great European City (Berlin), beauti-
    ful hotel and skyscraper tenements.
Footage.......6519.

Cast

The............................*Emil Jannings*
His Daughter....................*Mary Delschaft*
Her Bridegroom...................*Kurt Hiller*
His Aunt........................*Emile Kurz*
The Manager....................*Hans Unterkircher*
The Nightwatchman..............*George John*

Thumbnail Theme

A pompous old doorman, once big and powerful, is ruthlessly fired by the hotel manager. He sinks into despair. His daughter is married at this time, but his son-in-law turns him from the house when he hears of the old man's misfortune. Even the neighbors, once so proud to know the "great general," turn and mock him when they hear of his "disgrace." Under cover of night, he steals back to the hotel to return the gaudy uniform, now so useless to him. Sliding along the walls, he is horror-struck to behold the watchman. Feverishly he seizes the latter before he might pull his gun. In the flare of the watchman's light, he makes known his request. To his surprise, it is granted. There is no home for the old man now, other than in the lower depths of the hotel. He seems to sink deeper into despair from day to day. His son-in-law intimidates his own daughter from seeing him. Then comes a twist of fate, poverty is destroyed in what seems to be one blow. Love of many people, questionable though it might be, but love of a sort is scattered about, happily to a delightful climax in this masterpiece of human nature.

Copy of a rotogravure of Marlene Dietrich.

CHAPTER TWO

Color Photographs and Negatives

When "Becky Sharp" opened in 1935, it followed a year-long promotion campaign promising that "technicolor" would be as entertaining and "miraculous" as talkies. And it was! "Becky Sharp" was the first full-length feature movie to be made entirely in color. Although the colors were far from natural—sometimes too harsh, sometimes washed out, lacking subtlety most of the time—"technicolor" became a synonym for a new kind of movie experience that brought sunlight and vivid color into the darkened theater. The silver screen became a kaleidoscope.

Color was used in movies before "Becky Sharp," but only for a few moments at a time and then only by the use of tinting so that brilliant day was suggested by orange colors and deep night by blue. Tinted photographs from the first movies to use color tinting, made in 1918–1925, are extremely rare and historically very valuable. However, except for a few collectors and special historical archives, these are not in any real demand. Color from the movies from 1935 (when it all began) to the early 1940s (when every major studio had chosen its own style for color processing) is very highly prized by collectors.

The success of "technicolor," like the later success of cinerama, which involved specially manufactured wide-angle projection lenses and projectors, caused a wild rush among manufacturers to produce competing color equipment. The surge of interest in color movies brought about tremendous progress in color photography for both the professional and the amateur, making it possible, for the first time, for movie enthusiasts to see color reproductions of movie stars in magazines, newspapers, and prints suitable for framing and collecting.

Almost all of the color movie photographs and reproductions from before 1935 do not represent true color photography at all but are merely hand tinted. The hand-tinting process is a simple one involving not much more than the daubing of one or at most two colors onto a

43

print with a chalk-based paint by means of a watercolor brush. Printing two or even three hand-tinted photographs was technically easy and relatively inexpensive on regular lithographic presses. However, true color printing required costly presses, special paper, and techniques that were either too expensive or not readily available.

The first true color photographs of movie personalities began to appear in the "Sunday supplements" of newspapers. These supplement sections were called *rotogravure* sections because the color photographs used in them were printed by special printing presses called rotogravure presses. Once the popularity of color was established by the weekly rotogravures, the newsmagazines, fan magazines, monthlies, and all sorts of special publications began to show movie personalities in color. Although hand-tinted photographs have only a limited value and appeal, true color produced from 1935 to 1940 commands high prices, especially for the negatives.

Color from 1935 to 1940 is strikingly attractive, and while color after 1940 is technically better, the later photographs lack the rich mood and *movie sense* present in the best of the early color. This is due to the fact that the color photographs destined for use in the rotogravure section were taken in studios where much attention was given to preparation: make-up, lighting, position, suggestiveness of the movie theme, proper costuming, and props. There were not many good techniques (as we have these days) to touch up color negatives to correct errors. There was also the expectation that color photographs had to *do* more for the audience than color must do these days.

The earlier color photographs are very much like miniature movies arrested in one sequence. The entire story of the movie and the most attractive side of the movie personality had to be told in one photograph in which the color did not steal the scene but instead enhanced it as permanent entertainment. The clothing or costumes worn by the stars had to contrast satisfactorily with the prepared backdrop of the photo or there would be fuzziness in the final printed version. Special make-up had to be worn to make up for the fact that many stars look terrific in black-and-white photographs but tend to look pasty in color. The results were amazing. W.C. Fields (who made only black-and-white movies) appears in some color rotogravures, beautifully costumed as a character from a Dickens' novel, looking funnier and more vivacious than in most of the black-and-white films he played in. These color photographs are treasures of a great movie comedian and character actor, and the color brings him closer to the viewer and makes him more memorable at the same time.

It is difficult to resist acquiring this type of memorabilia. One hundred dollars is a reasonable price for a 12″ x 15″ rotogravure cover and if there are color negatives somewhere, someone is doing a marvelous job of keeping them hidden. They have never been offered for sale and it is entirely possible that the original negatives have been lost. The rotogravure printing process used at least four engraved plates, or separations as they are called, to make such a photo. While the film separations may be purchased for a few hundred dollars, the plates themselves are useless unless they are made to print on special presses and with special ink. Therefore, to duplicate such great color as the W.C. Fields cover would be prohibitively expensive for collectors. You can compare the excellence of a rotogravure like Fields' with earlier hand-tinted color or later hastily made but fuzzy covers to get a quick idea of why there are substantial differences in memorabilia prices even for material which seems, superficially, to be similar.

Many people have seen Bette Davis in her Academy Award winning "Jezebel." You may have seen it either when it premiered in 1938 or in one of the many re-releases on television. It is an outstanding movie and Bette Davis is at her very best. One of the great scenes in the movie occurs when Bette deliberately shocks her Southern friends and relatives by appearing at a very formal ball in a red gown. This moment is so powerful that most people who have seen the movie are convinced that they actually saw the famous red gown *in color*. This, of course, is not possible since "Jezebel" is entirely in black and white. The only mementos of the gown, in color, are in the lovely rotogravure reproductions of the scene.

The best of the rotogravure covers are those from the period 1935 to 1940, such as the covers of *Life* magazine or a sizeable number of the covers of the Sunday magazine section of *The New York Daily News*. The collector should be very careful in considering color covers because there are sharp differences in quality from issue to issue, since the color performance of even the better magazines was not consistent. Some issues are collectors' dreams, while others show double lips, fuzziness, faded eyes, lifeless poses, and visual flatness. Even with their flaws they are expensive because color photographs of the stars for the period from 1935 to 1940 are becoming impossible to find. Second and sometimes third preference will have to substitute in times of acute shortage. For example, I once spent weeks trying to find an outstanding negative of Claudette Colbert. The one I finally bought for one hundred and fifty dollars—a bargain—is very enjoyable, but a second preference. There were no better negatives to be found even for my top offer of five hundred dollars.

An average *Life* cover of a star in 1937 will command a modest price of forty dollars, but it will probably be worth two to three times this amount in a few years. Inferior quality color covers of *Life* are worth a dollar or possibly two. However, some of *Life*'s outstanding color covers are now bringing ninety to one hundred dollars. An important criterion for deciding whether a color cover is worth the price, is how effectively it captures a particular moment in a star's life and how, like the movies, it touches an emotional chord.

Negatives of color photographs enjoy a high value among collectors which is not found among other memorabilia. Excellent high quality copies of photographs may be made, in black and white or in color, and reduced or enlarged as well, for only a few dollars if the negative is a good one. Photos can then be sold or traded with other collectors or dealers. Negatives have a beauty in themselves. They can be enjoyed by holding them up to a good source of light. Changing light imparts changing moods to the negative, and these are reflected in the face of the movie personality, especially if the negative is a carefully made portrait. Color negatives of scenes, posed or unposed, are less exciting to look at since they do not vary as much with different sources of light. The wonderfully expressive face of Gary Cooper conveys different moods, ranging from strong self-confidence to brooding self-doubt, depending on the time of day you look at it and whether you hold it up to natural or artificial light. There are some color negatives that shouldn't change in mood; the way the photograph was taken is exactly the mood that should be evoked time and again. A very rare 8″ x 10″ color negative of Fred Astaire doesn't change at all, no matter what kind of lighting is used. Astaire's vibrant character and the dynamism of his total look as he is about to be transformed into dance seem to be permanently fixed in the negative.

Color negatives are very hard to find. They were originally made to be sent to magazine and newspaper editors to be used in promotional stories. Most were discarded after being used. Since the 1940s, the process used for printing color photographs has not relied on a negative, so the use of negatives in color is confined to a relatively brief period of time—another reason they are so scarce. Photographs in color or in black and white can now be transmitted electronically without any need for a negative at all. Whenever an editor needs a color photo for a story, he can obtain it in minutes via the telephone transmission system or he can have a 35mm slide delivered from one of numerous photographic libraries and archives, but these will be photographs of current personalities. Even editors of magazines have difficulty in obtaining high quality color photographs of movie personalities before 1940. A photo archive will charge from one-hundred-and-fifty to five hundred dollars for a one-time use of a color negative for a magazine or newspaper story. Color is one of the fastest disappearing memorabilia items, and collectors interested in it should be prepared for frustrations, high prices, and high profits.

Color negatives may be found in the same three standard·sizes as black-and-white photographs: 4″ x 6″, 5″ x 7″, and 8″ x 10″. The two larger sizes are in greater demand and are rarer than the 4″ x 6″s. Fewer of the 8″ x 10″s were made originally because of the higher cost of manufacture and processing. However, they are more enjoyable to handle and will produce contact copies and enlargements with greater fidelity of detail and color than the smaller sizes. Quality is important when a collector wishes to make a poster-size enlargement of a color negative.

As much as possible, collectors should avoid acquiring color negatives that have been made from color photographs or reproductions from rotogravure and magazine covers. You should also avoid negatives made from other negatives. The quality of copies of negatives is inferior and you should not allow them to get into your collection unless the subject itself is very important to your collection. The color of copies is really irritatingly bad, especially when you compare these copies with the rich color of the original negatives. If you have any doubts about whether a negative is an original or a copy, a quick way to find out is to hold the questionable one up to the light next to a negative you know is an original. It won't take more than a glance to see the difference. The copy will look like a pale imitation, unappealing even under strong light, with poor details and no depth whatever. Since any kind of color is costly, you should be sure that that which you allow into your collection is of good quality.

An excellent 8″ x 10″ color negative is one that has a terrific subject, rich color, no scratches, and is an original rather than a copy—and will take a long time to find but is well worth owning. The price should range from between three-hundred-and-fifty to five hundred dollars for that single sheet of hardened gelatin. Smaller-sized color negatives are proportionately less expensive. Color photographs or prints made from 8″ x 10″ original color negatives are less difficult to find than negatives and their price, depending on quality and subject, is between fifteen and twenty dollars. The owner of an excellent color negative can easily recover his investment by selling prints to other collectors, provided the other collectors are eager to own color. One of the main reasons many collectors avoid enlarging their collections of color is that so much effort and expense are required to develop a broad and interesting collection.

A substitute—satisfactory but not nearly as beautiful or, in the long run, as profitable—for color negatives is the 35mm slide. These tiny frames, usually 1″ x 1″ or 2″ x 2″ and mounted on cardboard as protection for handling or insertion into a slide projector, are not expensive—generally under ten dollars for stars after 1950. You can often get them free of charge by writing to the agent or publicist for the personality you are interested in and explaining that you are a collector. These slides do not make high quality enlargements and are not exciting to look at by holding them to the light. Many slides, however, will offer a delightful experience to anyone interested in the movies when shown on a good quality projector. The chief problem with 35mm slides is that they are not available as originals for personalities and scenes before 1950, so you cannot look forward to acquiring these low cost substitutes for old negatives for movies and stars of the 1930s and 1940s.

A good way for collectors to gauge the importance and scarcity of quality color is to look at many of the movie books published during the last few years that include color. You will find that the color range is limited and that, with few exceptions, the printing is less than satisfactory. When you find a movie book with beautiful color, it is definitely worth adding to your collection. If the color looks great in a movie book, you can be sure that tremendous effort went into discovering excellent negatives and that an equal effort went into excellent printing. The book is worth the price for the color photographs alone.

Prices for Color

Negatives	Average Price
8″ x 10″ vertical portraits	$150.00
8″ x 10″ action scene, posed	100.00
8″ x 10″ action scene, blow-up from frame of actual footage	75.00
8″ x 10″ made from another negative or from a color photo	50.00
4″ x 5″ vertical portrait	80.00
4″ x 5″ action scene, posed	50.00
4″ x 5″ action scene, blow-up from frame of actual footage	25.00
4″ x 5″ made from another negative or from a color photo	10.00
35mm framed transparency, portrait	10.00
35mm framed transparency, action scene	8.00
35mm framed transparency, copy made from actual footage	5.00
35mm framed transparency, news-type photo once used in a publication	50.00

Color Photographs	
Hand-tinted original with full credit and caption	10.00
Full-color original with credit and caption	15.00
Hand-tinted or full-color with credit and caption of a movie made in black and white	10.00–75.00
Full-color vertical portrait 8″ x 10″	12.00–20.00
Full-color copy from an inferior negative	5.00

Rotogravure	
Before 1930	10.00–30.00
1930–1935	10.00–20.00
1935–1940	5.00–10.00
After 1940	2.00–5.00

Magazine Covers and Inside Photographs	
Before 1930	10.00–20.00
1930–1935	10.00–50.00
1935–1940	10.00–25.00

1940–1950	5.00–10.00
After 1950	5.00

"Coming Attraction" Slides

Before 1920	40.00–50.00
1920–1925	50.00–100.00
1925–1930	75.00–200.00

COLOR
NEGATIVES

Rotogravure negative of Spencer Tracy.

Collection:

Sol Chaneles

8″ x 10″ original negative of Rita Hayworth.

Negative from a magazine cover showing
Judy Garland.

4″ x 5″ original negative of Barbra Streisand.

8" x 10" original negative
of Gary Cooper.

4" x 5" original negative
of Humphrey Bogart.

8″ x 10″ original negative of Fred Astaire.

AS EXCITING AS THE LANDING AT CASABLANCA

WARNER BROS.'
Sensational
Story of the City
that Rocked
the World!

HUMPHREY
BOGART
INGRID
BERGMAN
PAUL ('Now, Voyager')
HENREI[]

A SURPRISING CAST TO TELL A SUPER-SURPRISING STOR[]

"CASABLANCA"

HAL B. WALLIS PROD'N.

CLAUDE
RAINS ·
CONRAD
VEIDT ·
SYDNEY
GREENSTREET ·
PETER
LORRE ·
Directed by
MICHAEL CURTIZ

Screen Play by Julius J. & Philip G. Epstein and Howard Koch · From a Play by Murray Burnett and Joan Alison · Music by Max Steiner

Lobby Card, 11″ x 14″.   *Collection: Gene Andrewski.*

CHAPTER THREE

Posters, Lobby Cards, and Inserts

The first posters to advertise movies appeared during World War I, 1914–1918. Governments produced movie posters to advertise films showing the nation's preparedness for war. The movies themselves were usually short documentaries or newsreels made with lots of derring-do on the part of pilots and news photographers. Posters for feature movies did not begin to appear until the 1920s, and posters in color and in standard sizes did not make their appearance until the late 1920s. Until color posters became popular ways to publicize movies, most outdoor advertising for movies was done by means of handbills or "flyers," billboards made of heavy pasteboard that had to be tacked into place, or large sheets (or post bills as they were first called) that were pasted into place. These bills of varying sizes were originally printed in bold letters with black ink. Line drawings or a photograph were occasionally added. The very first announcements for movies were simply notices printed on advertising bills stating that at the conclusion of a vaudeville show a movie would be shown. As feature movies became popular, handbills and large printed post bills began to advertise exclusively for movies. The earliest printed posters are very interesting to collectors of the history of movies or advertising or printing, but they have very little appeal or value to collectors of movie memorabilia. The chief reason, which anyone can see at a glance, is that the earlier printed bills are neither beautiful to look at nor do they evoke a particular movie or the performers we invariably think about when we think about the movies.

Once posters became popular collectors' items, they began to appear almost everywhere as a form of everyday art: in hotel lobbies, on restaurant walls, in clothing shops, and in recreation areas, using the original posters in color or enormous enlargements in black and white. The popularity of movie posters as public art has not in any way diminished their appeal to collectors.

The first posters made expressly for the movies—using movie themes and showing movie personalities as part of the poster concept—were printed in color. At this time, movies were entirely made in black and white except for the insertion of a few seconds of color. The first feature length color movie appeared in 1935, so for at least ten years movie-goers were entering darkened theaters with their impressions of color furnished by the vividly colored posters. Posters that appeared before sound took over the movies carried dialogue balloons set between or above the main characters of the movie. Such snippets of dialogue gave movie-goers a sense of sound, even though the movies themselves were silent. By the 1940's, sound and color were being widely used in the movies and an entirely new method of advertising by means of posters had to be developed. Unfortunately, the development was a faint imitation of the earlier posters. The finest movie posters are, therefore, those that were made between 1920 and 1940; the best and most memorable of those produced during this twenty-year period are the ones that appeared during the golden decade from 1930 to 1940. It was an extraordinary achievement for the poster artists of this period to have us remember "City Lights" (1931) for its *sound* even though it is one of Charlie Chaplin's great *silent* movies, and to have us remember the fanatastic *color* of Busby Berkeley's "Roman Scandals" (1933) even though it was filmed entirely in *black and white*. The great movie posters have a magical quality like the magic of the movies they were made to promote. If a movie isn't memorable, it is likely that the poster art for it is forgettable as well.

Movie posters were developed as part of an advertising and publicity campaign formulated by production and distribution companies. Every promotional device that the companies made was described in press books distributed to local theater managers to help them choose the kind of materials they wanted to use to get box-office results. The material itself, tons of it over the course of a year, was shipped to regional exchanges. These exchanges were storage houses for reels of film that were going to be shown or shipped to another city or another movie house within a city and for vast quantities of movie advertising materials. The exchanges handled the local booking for a movie and also handled the distribution of advertising and promotional materials. In principle, the exchange was supposed to charge a theater manager for advertising materials such as posters. The charge was either on a purchase or a rental basis. The amount was very small, anywhere from two cents for a small poster to twenty-five cents for a very large one, and this token amount represented only the satisfaction of a legal requirement to the effect that the producing company could not influence a theater manager's choice of movie for his house by providing free advertising materials.

From the mid-1920s to the mid-1950s (when the big studios began to disappear), there were thirty movie exchanges in the United States—from Albany to Seattle, from Los Angeles to Altanta—and in every foreign capital of the world there was at least one exchange to handle American-made movies. These exchanges had to handle tremendous quantities of material. For example, a typical exchange had to handle material for anywhere from three hundred to six hundred movie houses and anywhere from two hundred to three hundred movies a year. When a movie was taken out of circulation in the region served by an exchange, the exchange manager was not eager to keep the leftover material in his warehouse. He gave away some to those movie enthusiasts in the area who, even in the early days of the movies, were avid collectors of memorabilia. He sold most of it to paper scrap dealers to be reduced to pulp for common pasteboard. Every few months, the exchange warehouse would begin to bulge with leftover posters, inserts, lobby cards, special promotional materials made for tie-in events, parade floats, novelties for store displays, and banners for festivals and conventions. When the surplus was no longer manageable, the materials would be baled, shredded, and reduced to pulp. On a smaller scale, this is just about what happened in movie houses all over the country and in foreign movie houses. Within a few days after a film had ended its run, the posters, inserts, lobby cards, stills, and banners that had been rented, bought, or borrowed were either sent back to the exchange warehouse or destroyed. Some of the materials, of course, came into the possession of budding collectors. There were also thrifty managers who couldn't stand to see anything destroyed and who stored the materials in a storage room of the theater. There were other managers who simply gave the colorful material away to anyone willing to carry it off. In this way, poster materials were rescued from total loss. Some of the people around the country who are supplying collectors and dealers with material have no recollection of how they or members of their families came into possession of posters and other movie materials. Many say with a smile that the materials turned up in an attic, the back of a garage, or in a storage room. Many of us have reason to be grateful for the thriftiness of managers past who couldn't bear to destroy beautiful objects.

One of America's leading early collector-dealers of movie memorabilia, Mark Ricci, is considered the pioneer movie poster collector and the rescuer of a large part of the poster art that has been bought up in outstanding poster collections. The chief poster collector-dealers of America acknowledge Mark, who has been collecting movie materials for most of his life, as a leading authority on movie posters. With awe and a bit of envy, the collectors tell the following story about Mark. While traveling through Canada during the late 1950s in search of movie materials, Mark noticed a newspaper advertisement placed by a regional exchange. It offered tens of thousands of posters, inserts, lobby cards, and black-and-white stills to anyone willing to pay the cost of carting the material away from the warehouse. The shipping cost: ten thousand dollars. Much of this material has now entered collections throughout the world, and in the course of sorting, classifying, and arranging his materials so that they might be accessible to collectors and dealers, Mark trained some of the most prominent movie memorabilia dealers and dealer-collectors in the United States.

Jack Banning, without question the leading collector-dealer of movie posters, has moved away from the general sale of posters to a very selective business in rare and beautiful posters. Although he carries a good assortment of fine posters and lobby cards, his main activity is finding and mounting rare posters for sale to discerning, well-to-do private collectors who will pay between a few hundred and a few thousand dollars for a movie poster. Banning's memorabilia shop includes a remarkably well-organized gallery for showing posters, and he makes plenty of time available to collectors to explain the hows and whys of poster collecting. He has set high standards for other collector-dealers to emulate.

A rule that applies primarily to movie posters (including lobby cards and inserts) is that material from the period from 1930 to 1940 is not only the most vivid, interesting, and beautiful, but because it is so scarce it is also the most expensive to acquire and the most profitable to sell. For example, a first release poster for "Frankenstein" (1931) is selling for five hundred dollars, and there are literally thousands of collectors who would pay a premium to get a mint copy of this collector's rarity.

Another reason the pre-1950s posters are so attractive to collectors is that posters made after 1950 lack the magical artistic quality of the earlier posters.

Different Sizes of Posters, Lobby Cards, and Inserts

When architects designed movie theaters, they planned spaces to exhibit one, two, or more sheet posters which were each 27″ x 41″. These dimensions were made necessary by the lithographic printing beds which had been built to produce printed sheets of a standard size— 27″ x 41″. Theaters that did not have cases to accommodate cards or frames to hold inserts often made use of these materials by placing them on stands and tripods. The following figures give some of the different sizes.

Item	Standard Size	Average Size
One-half sheet poster	27″ x 41″	
One sheet poster	22″ x 28″	
Two to Six sheet posters	2 to 6 times 27″ x 41″	
Lobby card—A		8″ x 10″
Lobby card—B		10″ x 14″
Lobby card—C		15″ x 22″
Inserts (sometimes also called title cards)		6″ x 10″, 8″ x 10″, or 8″ x 14″

After a theater manager received the press book from the regional exchange, he would place an order for the materials that best fit his lobby and outside display areas. A great deal of attention was given by the artists to producing a lively variety of materials so that the package a manager ordered would permit him to mount an original and interesting display.

Some collectors have built unusual collections of complete display packages. A collection along these lines is considerably more valuable than the individual items added together. The typical display package a manager ordered was likely to include:

1   1 sheet (27″ x 41″)
1   4 sheet or 6 sheet for the neighborhood billboard
2   3 sheets for display on the theater's outdoor wall frames
8   lobby cards
4   inserts

In addition to the basic display package, a manager could select a "set" of lobby cards. The "set," as designed by the artist, generally con-

One-half-sheet poster.   *Collection: Yesterday.*

One of the most popular inserts of all time, 11″ x 14″ horizontal.
Collection: Jerry Ohlinger.

Lobby card.   *Collection: Gene Andrewski.*

Lobby card.   *Collection: Gene Andrewski.*

Lobby card. *Collection: Gene Andrewski.*

One-sheet poster. *Collection: Gene Andrewski.*

One-sheet poster. *Collection: Yesterday.*

One-sheet poster. *Collection: Hake.*

THE IMMENSELY POPULAR
SERIALS POSTERS

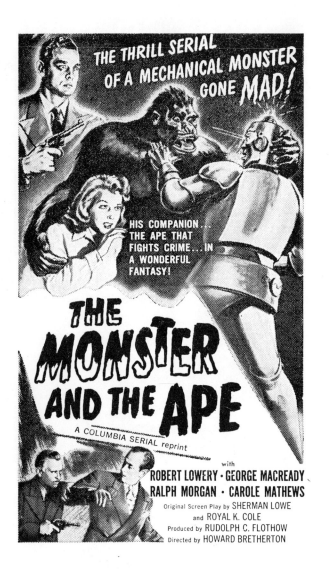

THE THRILL SERIAL
OF A MECHANICAL MONSTER
GONE MAD!

HIS COMPANION...
THE APE THAT
FIGHTS CRIME...IN
A WONDERFUL
FANTASY!

THE MONSTER AND THE APE

A COLUMBIA SERIAL reprint

with
ROBERT LOWERY · GEORGE MACREADY
RALPH MORGAN · CAROLE MATHEWS
Original Screen Play by SHERMAN LOWE
and ROYAL K. COLE
Produced by RUDOLPH C. FLOTHOW
Directed by HOWARD BRETHERTON

THE
Most Sensational
SKY-SERIAL
EVER MADE!
...Amazing air ad-
ventures...as heroes
battle spies in the sky!

SKY RAIDERS

with
DONALD WOODS
BILLY HALOP
ROBT. ARMSTRONG
KATHRYN ADAMS
EDWARD CIANNELLI
BILL CODY, Jr.

12 Thrill-Powered Chapters

sisted of eight lobby cards. Each card told a portion of the story and showed at least one—but rarely more than two—of the leading performers in the film at a dramatic moment. Collections of lobby cards "sets" are becoming increasingly valuable because they are difficult to assemble, although somewhat less difficult than a complete display package. A mounted "set" of lobby cards makes an extremely interesting and appealing decoration.

Signed Posters and Serial Numbers

Poster art began in Europe around 1876, and from the beginning the artist signed his name on the lithographic stone or plate. Since posters were produced in relatively limited quantities, the European lithographer also numbered many of the sheets that came from his presses. Except in rare instances, movie posters in America were not autographed or given identifying numbers until the 1970s.

Among the rare instances of signed movie posters are those for "Song of Bernadette" and "Stagecoach." The poster artwork for both films was done by Norman Rockwell and his signature appears on the posters. The signature is printed on the poster and not personally autographed. A poster that is both signed *and* autographed would have considerable value, especially if the autograph was affixed at the time of first release. Although collectors tell about purchases of such rarities, the transactions have been private and no information has been made available about the details of the sales.

Poster art for the movies was primarily anonymous, but this did not stop some proud artists from rebelling by subtly weaving their signature into the artwork.

There is no certain way to determine how many posters were printed for a given movie or which lithography house printed them. Nearly all re-release posters are identified by the letter "R," which stands for re-release. The "R" is followed by two digits that stand for the year of re-release and this is followed by three digits that indicate the order of release. Hence, serial R-54-231 indicates a 1954 re-release which was the distributor's 231st film released that year.

In buying posters, collectors should be very careful to make sure that they are not paying first release prices for re-release materials. Re-release posters may be purchased for a fraction of the prices of first releases. The serial numbers for re-releases are always printed or stamped on the lower border of the poster, and if this portion of the poster is destroyed or marred, there is a good chance that it is *not* a first release.

Due to the growth of popularity of movie posters among collectors during the past ten years, many dealers and collectors have gotten retired actors and actresses as well as producers and directors to autograph a poster for a movie made thirty or more years ago. While such recently autographed posters have some value for collectors, their value depends on whether the autographs are authentic. In making such a purchase, a collector should expect to get a certificate of authenticity.

Current Movie Poster Prices

The prices of movie posters, lobby cards, and inserts will vary greatly depending on their condition, aesthetic appeal, and historical importance. Price is also influenced by how much collectors want a particular poster. Until 1970, a two-sheet poster of the Marx Brothers in "Horsefeathers" could be bought for $7. In 1975, the poster sold for $12,000. For ten years the movie rebel-hero James Dean had a strong following and although there was a limited supply of poster materials about him, prices rarely went over $25 for a single sheet. Increased interest in Dean and in posters pushed the price of the Dean poster to $100 in 1976. The average price of inserts in 1970 was $5, but by 1976 many had gone up to $500. Because many new collectors wanted Humphrey Bogart posters, a one-sheet "Sierra Madre" brought $1,500 in 1976. It could have been bought in 1970 for $100. There are still many fine posters that can be acquired by collectors for under $25. Prices are not likely to go down, so a carefully built collection based on a modest budget will represent a cautious investment.

The following table will give you an idea of current prices for different types of posters.

Sample Prices According to Year and Personality

All material is first release and in fine but not mint condition, nearly always with two folds.

Year	Subject	One Sheet 27" x 41"	Lobby Cards and Inserts
1925	Lon Chaney, Sr.	$ 90.00	$ 25.00
1930	Rudolph Valentino	175.00	15.00

1935	Clark Gable	225.00	10.00
1940	James Cagney	50.00	15.00
1945	Gary Cooper	40.00	10.00
1950	Orson Welles	35.00	8.00
1955	James Dean	25.00	5.00
1960	Spencer Tracy	15.00	10.00
1965	Marlon Brando	17.00	5.00
1970	The Beatles	55.00	10.00
1975	James Caan	10.00	2.00

Average Prices for Poster Materials

Posters	*Average Price*
All Through the Night	$ 35.00
Always Goodbye	27.00
Anchors Aweigh	20.00
Beyond the Forest	22.00
Boom	15.00
Bringing Up Baby	35.00
Chinatown	20.00
Cleopatra	40.00
Country Girl	28.00
From Russia With Love	18.00
I'll Cry Tomorrow	40.00
Gentlemen Prefer Blondes	60.00
The Godfather	22.00
The Heiress	40.00
Man of a Thousand Faces	17.00
Picture of Dorian Gray	22.00
Miss Sadie Thompson	45.00
Sayonara	30.00
Sign of the Cross	25.00
Song of the Islands	27.00
A Star Is Born	55.00
Susan & God	75.00
Sweet Birth of Youth	18.00
They Met in Bombay	70.00
Yellow Sky	60.00

and a few rarities:

Camille	4,500.00
Citizen Kane	1,200.00

Phantom of the Opera	2,000.00
Naughty Marietta	300.00

Lobby Cards (11" x 14")

(Often sold in a set of eight cards at a price slightly less than eight times the price of one.)

Ace Drummond	25.00
Arabian Nights	35.00
The Belle of New York	12.00
Blood of Fu Manchu	50.00
Broadway Melody of 1940	30.00
The Bullfighter	7.00
The Creature Walks Among Us	22.00
Danger of Wheels	28.00
Easter Parade	20.00
Enter the Dragon	15.00
Godzilla	32.00
Hats Off	15.00
Hopalong Cassidy Rides Again	35.00
Horror of Dracula	30.00
Invisible Boy	25.00
Joan of Arc	12.00
Lost Patrol	40.00
Man From Planet X	30.00
The Man in the Iron Mask	22.00
The Prince and the Showgirl	32.00
Rollerball	5.00
Seventh Voyage of Sinbad	30.00
Sleeping Beauty	45.00
This Island Earth	45.00
2001: A Space Odyssey	12.00
Undercurrent	10.00
The Wolf Man	30.00

Autographed portrait of Jean Harlow, affectionately signing "me"
to her grandmother.   *Collection: Gene Andrewski.*

CHAPTER FOUR

"3-D"*: Decorative Memorabilia, Curios, and Knicknacks

Collecting Americana is becoming an increasingly important pursuit for a growing number of Americans as well as foreigners who find the combination of untrained skills, pure American themes, and joyous outlook to be irresistible. Modern Americana has become as appealing and in demand as eighteenth- and early nineteenth-century carvings, furniture, quilts, and other everyday objects which were made by farmers and small-town craftsmen. Some very unique Americana (such as the cigar store Indian, dry sinks, weathervanes, and whirligigs), which have been appreciated and collected for a long time, is now being joined by newly-made braided rugs, wicker chairs, and picture frames. As we discover our own artistic impulses, past and present, and the common objects of home, play, and work that are made uncommonly interesting and beautiful through our experience and labors, the scope of cherished Americana is being enlarged.

One of the areas of Americana that has been winning increased interest is the wide range of bric-a-brac, toys, curios, or knicknacks (call the objects what you will), all of which were movie-related materials. There are literally hundreds of different kinds of "3–D" decorative movie memorabilia and the demand for them is becoming so intense that prices are, as a rule, unreasonably high. A lovely silver birch 9" x 6" x 2" candy box made in 1939 and burnished with a scene from "Gone With the Wind" sells for ninety dollars; an ingenious and colorful tin toy of Eddie Cantor that rolls its eyes, opens its mouth, waves its hands, and bows its legs sells for three-hundred-and-fifty dollars; a metal beer tray with the hand-painted likeness of almost any movie personality from the

*"3-D" is the term most often used by collectors.

early 1930s sells for between seventy-five and one hundred dollars; and personality piggy banks, mantelpiece clocks with metal bas-reliefs of movie scenes, personality wrist watches, and cufflinks are bringing fantastic prices.

Part of the explanation for these unusually high prices is the fact that decorative movie memorabilia have become part of the very popular nostalgia style or fashion. A more important explanation is that the objects are beautiful in themselves as well as excitingly evocative of the movies and movie personalities they portray, and as a result are an important part of our own experience. Seldom in one lifetime do the common objects of our growing up become rare for reasons of economics, technology, history, or whatever, and, just as important, become widely recognized as things of beauty and enduring value genuinely worthy of careful, thoughtful collecting. In my childhood the lids of ice cream "Dixie" cups that carried affectionate photographs of the great stars of the period were important playthings; images for summertime daydreams which were eventually discarded. How nice it is to see and own a Jeannette MacDonald lid, and enjoy once again the romance and adventure that filled childhood days with pleasure and entered in important ways into the play of children.

The extent and quality of decorative movie memorabilia would not have become as quickly and widely known as they did had it not been for the phenomenal popularity of outdoor garage sales and flea markets. For the very small fee charged by organizers of these markets, anyone with objects to sell can make them available to an eager public. Attics, cellars, garages, and storerooms that in the past were emptied of long-forgotten objects only after spring cleaning or when the house was sold and the furnishings auctioned off are now being regularly sifted over in order to find objects that will bring good prices at the outdoor markets. On a pleasant spring or summer day an outdoor flea market in New Brunswick, New Jersey, or Kutztown, Pennsylvania, will attract several hundred weekend dealers and several thousand prospective buyers. Some very large flea markets have acquired former farm acreage in order to make parking space available for the three to five thousand cars of the customers visiting at a given time. The garage sales and flea markets are likely to be, for a few more years, the best possible source for building up collections of decorative movie memorabilia that are varied and not prohibitively expensive. Although most of the flea market dealers are not in business on a full-time basis, it is fair to say that they have a professional and businesslike attitude and will stand up for their merchandise if a purchaser is dissatisfied for good cause. One of the problems a collector will have with flea market dealers, however, is that while the dealer is ethical, it may be virtually impossible to locate him if you want to return the merchandise you have bought. Or it may simply be too expensive to go through the trouble of returning an object you're not satisfied with. The best way to avoid the problem while taking advantage of the relatively reasonable prices of the flea markets is to know as much as possible about the object you are considering before buying it. You will also be helping yourself to avoid costly mistakes by having a pretty good feeling in advance about the probable market value of your prospective purchase.

Specialized movie memorabilia shops are beginning to open up around the country but, for the present, although they deal in movie materials they may only carry a small number of decorative objects and not have current and useful shopping information. The same is true of most antique and Americana shops which have a small number of movie memorabilia curios and knicknacks which were acquired by the dealer because they were made during a period that the dealer knows well. However, the dealer is usually not as fully informed as he would like to be about movie objects. In time, this will be corrected so that collectors will have central places to see pieces and compare quality and price.

Although cheap imitators of movie curios and bric-a-brac are not likely to make copies of dishware because it is too expensive, they are copying (and doing it badly) club membership buttons. A collector can be fairly sure of getting an authentic dish but will have a hard time deciding whether a button is authentic or not. Once you begin to see enough examples of particular kinds of decorative memorabilia you will find yourself with a "sixth sense" about authenticity as well as quality. It is important to see as many objects as you can and to make comparisons, otherwise you will find yourself—especially at a time when decorative memorabilia prices are inflated—with too many high-priced collectibles, many of which will be of doubtful authenticity. You can help yourself acquire memorabilia of quality, interest, and value by letting dealers in collectibles and friends know of your interest in movie memorabilia. You will often find them drawing your attention to good prospects in places you would not normally have gone. I came upon a gem of a 1936 Shirley Temple wrist watch in excellent working condition—

a beautiful silver-plated work of art—in, of all places, a used furniture shop that also specialized in selling the paintings and carvings of the Northwest Canadian Indians! I would not have wandered into such a place had it not been for a good friend who did and who recalled my interest in movie memorabilia.

Decorative movie memorabilia, bric-a-brac, curios, and knicknacks were originally made to take advantage of the tremendous public interest in movies. Originally, the objects were souvenirs, premiums that were given away by theater operators or neighborhood merchants, door prizes, things that could be won at fairs and carnivals, and a dizzying variety of delightful things that didn't cost much, were not expected to last very long, and gave much pleasure to young and old alike.

These decorative objects were generally made by individual manufacturers who obtained a license from a movie production company to reproduce the likeness of a movie star or a scene from a movie on anything from an article of clothing to a pencil. However, there were many manufacturers who made these objects without the consent of the movie production company. Since the pirate or "bootleg" edition was likely to have been made in a hurry and without much genuine interest in providing a good likeness of a star or a clear image of a movie scene, you can often tell the licensed from the bootleg by the better quality of the licensed version. The same is true of original plaster casts of movie personalities such as Laurel and Hardy in 10″ to 12″ statuettes which were hand-painted and usually weighted at the base. These plaster casts were popular prizes at country fairs and amusement parks, and are now being widely imitated and sold at prices as high as the forty-five-year-old originals. Many other objects, such as coins, stamps, doorstops, bottles, and toilet accessories were sometimes made by companies that were subsidiaries of the movie production studios. These objects were distributed as part of a sales campaign for a store or company that tied in its advertising with the promotion for a movie. These objects are especially vivid and appealing; they are also hard to imitate, which is one reason why you can detect a copy from the real thing.

There are ten basic kinds of decorative movie memorabilia. Each may be collected as a specialized activity within the field, or as part of an even more specialized interest in antiques or Americana. Toys from the movies may be collected as a specialized pursuit or because you are also interested in old toys or in American handcraft objects of a certain period. There are specialized areas even within the category of toys; for example, there are movie toys that move (the wind-up kind), metal toys, wooden toys, and other special categories.

Ten Basic Kinds of Decorative Movie Memorabilia Objects

1. Toys

Some of the most delightful toys that can be found are wind-up toys of great movie performers which, when released, begin to *act* in the manner of the performer. A Charlie Chaplin tramp toy, a tin wind-up standing about 4″ high, will waddle forward, turn around, and lift his bowler hat in a gentle gesture of politeness. Another is a robot-like creature which resembles Boris Karloff in the role of Frankenstein's monster which walks clumsily while tilting his head from left to right and raising his arms to seize a victim. There's a splendid Tom Mix astride his stallion who, each time he pulls the reins to make his horse rear, raises his six-shooter into the air.

Many companies produced miniature sets of playing cards as premiums for their products. The face of the playing card contained, in addition to lightly colored numbers and suit signs, an excellent photograph of a movie actor or actress. The back of the card contained a lively synopsis of one of the best known movies of the actor or actress up to that time, along with a brief career biography. It sometimes took months for the purchaser to buy enough of the product to assemble a fifty-two card set, particularly a set that contained no duplicates; a fifty-two card set with fifty-two different actors and actresses and screen stories is a rarity.

Special playing card sets were made for westerns, detective stories, and costume historical adventures, and there are sets in the "giant" dimensions, 4″ x 6″ and 7″ x 9″, and some novelty sets—suitable for framing—that are 9″ x 12″. Until the fashion for playing card premiums ended around 1938, a western film fan might have amassed a collection of cards for every western movie made since 1910 and every western star who acted in them. For the miniatures, there are about sixteen different sets of playing cards featuring westerns and they are worth, as a collection of playing card sets, about $300.00.

2. Tableware

Among the most popular curios in this category are bottle stoppers made in the shape of a movie personality, especially one with easily recognizable, easy-to-caricature facial features, such as John Barrymore. Some stoppers, made of glazed, richly colored pottery, show the movie-radio comedian Joe Penner with his celebrated duck, or the wide-mouthed Joe E. Brown. These objects, along with similar utensils such as corkscrews, are mounted on corks or sturdy wooden handles. They are becoming increasingly hard to find, while costs are skyrocketing. Other memorabilia in the tableware category include dishes with borders garlanded in themes strongly suggestive of a movie, surrounding a portrait of a celebrated movie personality, usually in costume. Among the more durable and valuable tableware are pieces (entire 6-, 8-, or 10-piece sets are incredibly rare) made by various Wedgewood manufacturers in the unmistakable off-white and fluted edge Wedgewood style.

From time to time, you will be able to uncover a dinner platter that has, in addition to other decorative features, a cameo-sized medallion baked on the edge. These platters are unusually beautiful and lasting. Although tableware manufacturers generally made sets featuring one movie star, there are some individual pieces, suggesting that some manufacturers of premium dinnerware made sets which included a variety of stars from one major movie or one star in many different poses. Tableware items in porcelain, glass, or pottery are scarce as single pieces. Sets such as a matched cup and saucer are fantastically rare. This is surprising because during the early 1930s, when such premiums were popular ways to attract movie customers, millions of them were made.

Movie personality cutlery, like dishes, may be found as single pieces or, with considerable difficulty, in sets. A complete set of movie personality silverplate is a rarity of rarities in this category and will command at least $1000 for an eight-setting service. The most appealing and interesting items are embossed or engraved with a star's likeness and autograph, and have a decorative garland suggesting a movie theme.

3. Jewelry

The most varied category of knicknacks is jewelry. It is also the category with the widest price range—from a few pennies for a recent personality pin to several hundred dollars for a character wrist watch which was made in small quantities to commemorate a premiere. Among the most popular jewelry items are personality wrist watches. Since these novelty watches were mainly intended for small children, the most common personalities are Disney characters and some western stars as well as movie animals such as Lassie. It was not important to make the watches with good time-keeping movements or durable metalwork. The result is that most of these novelty watches are overpriced when compared to specially made wrist watches that still keep accurate time and are made with durable metal and good workmanship.

Other jewelry items include clothing accessories, such as tie clasps, lapel buttons, keychains, belt buckles, and ornate coat buttons. These items are available in abundance and generally cost under three dollars.

4. Boxes

Candy shops often tied in the sale of candy featuring movie themes on the boxes to the opening of a movie. Since the types of candy shops that sold candy in permanent boxes of wood and metal were found only in certain cities or in certain regions, relatively few boxes were made and only for a short time to tie in with promotion for an opening.

As a result, any kind of movie personality or movie theme boxes will remain very rare—unless the thousands of people who still use them as sewing boxes or places to store stamps or coins are ready to offer them for sale to collectors. A great deal of attention went into the decoration of these boxes and almost all of this effort was by hand. These boxes are truly an original art form.

5. Figurines

Usually made of porcelain, hand-painted plaster, glazed clay, or molded glass, these ever-popular objects are being increasingly copied from the "original casts," according to some advertisements. Possibly. However, a comparison between the delicately made and lovingly painted or finished originals with the less-than-satisfactory copies suggests that the molds are *not* the original ones. Figurines ranged in size from two inches to close to twenty inches. Some of them were completely painted when they were given away at a movie house entrance or at a fair, and some were given out with a card stating that a coloring set could be bought so that the figurine could be hand-painted by the owner. The most effective figurines are those showing movie personalities in costume from a particular movie. The owner who was able to get or be given figurines of other stars and principals from the same movie was quite lucky. The stars and co-stars, in figurine, from a costume romance of 1932 would be a fabulous group for any collection.

6. Decals

Two types of decals were very popular during the 1920s and 1930s: the color transfer decal and the film transfer decal. The first type had to be wet or moistened and applied to an object, whereupon a dye with a movie personality or scene would be transferred to the surface. With special care, the application of heat from a pressing iron might result in the successful transfer of the pattern to wood or cloth. Most kids who bought a color transfer decal with a candy at a Saturday afternoon matinee simply moistened the decal and applied the color to a hand or forearm, washing it away in the evening. For many kids, having Edward G. Robinson printed on your wrist for an afternoon was an immense treat. The film transfer method involved wetting the decal to activate a coating of cement or glue which, if quickly placed on an object, would result in the permanent transfer of the decoration. Glass tumblers were the most popular object to receive movie decals and some families had full sets with many different movie stars on them. Attractive decals are hard to find, but if you do find a package of mint decals it is likely to be a full set of twenty stars. Some collectors have been able to hold off the temptation to transfer a decal until they have collected enough of them to decide whether to apply them to a set of tumblers, dishes, boxes, or other objects.

7. Coins and Medallions

Except for special commemorative coins and medallions struck for a particular movie personality to honor him for his contributions to a particular club or film society, most coins and medallions are souvenir or premium items. They are attractive to own but take a long time to collect, since they have all but disappeared.

8. Post Cards

There are a rather large number of general post card collectors in the United States, but very few of them have maintained specialized collections of movie personality post cards. As a result, the cards are rare and valuable. They were originally produced by subsidiaries of movie companies to be mailed to fan club members, or to be mailed by the thousands to people in localities where a new movie was about to open. These were inexpensive and attractive ways of getting an advertising message into someone's hands in his own home. The original cards were produced from printing plates made directly from a studio portrait negative, so the cards have the same magical quality as the movie itself. Because original postal cards are rare, present-day manufacturers of movie item novelties are printing up post cards made not from original photographs, negatives, or old printing plates but from duplicates of duplicates of movie stills. The quality leaves much to be desired. Even though the newly made cards feature old-time favorite movies of the silent era or the 1930s, they should not be mistaken for the fine old cards which are more valuable.

9. School Supplies

Surprisingly, very little remains of the prodigious quantities of school supplies that were manufactured with delightful movie themes. Some of the prices being asked for these objects seem unreasonably high, but the objects are extremely nostalgic, entertaining, and highly decorative and, in small quantities, worth the exorbitant prices being asked. Very few Americans grew up without extensive contact with school supplies carrying movie themes and these still strike a warm, responsive chord in nearly everyone. Rulers with western themes, pencil sharpeners in the shape of a favored cartoon character, pads containing photographs along with story sketches and biographical information, and pencils tipped with a shaped rubber eraser in the form of a well-known star are just a few of the great variety in this category.

10. Other Knicknacks

Matchbook covers, paper silhouettes, ice cream "Dixie" lids, buttons, compasses, pen knives, stamps, and calendars are only a few of the large number of other knicknacks.

Sample Prices for 3–D Movie Memorabilia

Item	Average Price
Player's cards	$12.00–15.00 per set of 52 cards
Playing cards with scenes, portraits, and captions	$15.00–20.00 per set of 52 cards
Tin wind-up toys	$40.00–300.00
Personality watches	50.00–150.00
Personality piggy banks	35.00–75.00
Individual spoons, knives, tableware items	10.00–20.00
Post cards	10.00–20.00
Paperweights	10.00–20.00

Tumblers with decals	5.00–15.00
Banners, burgees	15.00–50.00
Insert frames	200.00–350.00
Standees (3″ x 4″ average)	300.00–400.00
Figurines (from 2″ to 18″)	25.00–75.00
Metal buttons	5.00–25.00
Sets of metal buttons (set of 6 "Wizard of Oz" or 8 "Gone With the Wind")	50.00–150.00
Costume jewelry	15.00–100.00
Novelty ties, ribbons, belts, suspenders	15.00–25.00
Serving trays	35.00–85.00
Dixie Cup lids	5.00–20.00
Animated items	
cells	20.00–250.00
models	100.00–300.00
original sketches	50.00–350.00
Animated toys and dolls (not mechanical)	25.00–50.00
Coloring books	2.00–35.00
Miscellaneous personality objects: brushes, pencil sharpeners, boxes, pads	10.00–50.00
Movie theater memorabilia: seats, decorative plaques, brass railings with studio or theater plaques, award plaques	100.00–500.00
Souvenir programs	25.00–50.00
Punch boards	15.00–20.00

"Homes of the Stars" postcard.   *Collection: Sol Chaneles.*

"3-D"

Tarzan puzzle.   *Collection: Hake.*

Chaplin toy.   *Collection: Hake.*

Three Little Pigs game.   *Collection: Hake.*

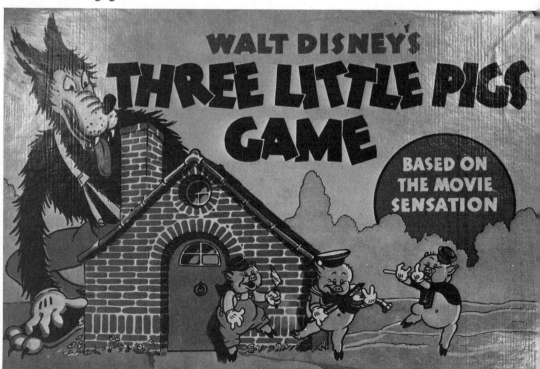

Elizabeth Taylor cut-out doll.
Collection: Hake.

Shirley Temple postcard.
Collection: Sol Chaneles.

Buttons.   *Collection: Hake.*

Giant champagne-glass bed from "What a Way to Go."

Shirley Temple's toys from "Captain January."

English perambulator from "Heaven Can Wait."

Marilyn Monroe's oval chaise from "Let's Make Love."

Tyrone Power resting on a prop chair frequently used in films of the 1930's.

The royal throne from "The King and I."

Frequently used horse-drawn gypsy caravan.

Model of galleon used in "Pirates of the Tortugas."

Horse-drawn bus from "Hello Dolly."

Sleigh with bob runners from "One in a Million."

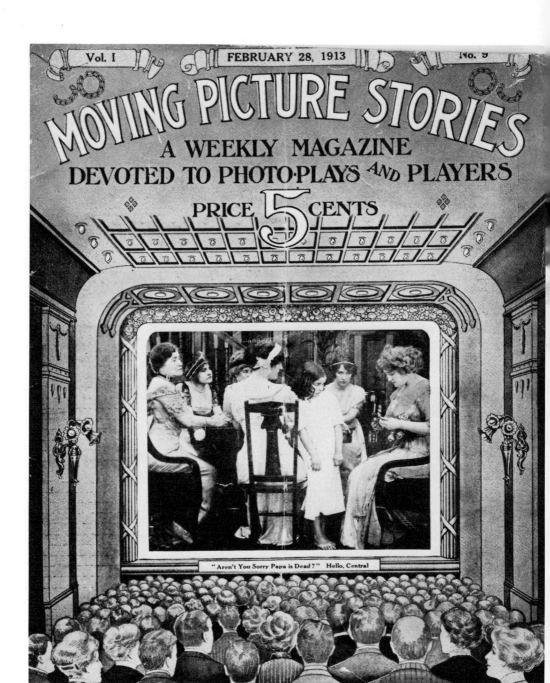

Vol. I   FEBRUARY 28, 1913   No. 9

MOVING PICTURE STORIES

A WEEKLY MAGAZINE
DEVOTED TO PHOTO·PLAYS AND PLAYERS
PRICE 5 CENTS

"Aren't You Sorry Papa is Dead?"   Hello, Central

CHAPTER FIVE

Fan Magazines (Fanzines)

By 1980, collectors will be paying from one hundred to two hundred dollars for a movie fan magazine that sold for ten cents in 1930. It will be worth the cost, especially if the magazine has been protected from weathering, folds, and tears. Some of the old, rare fanzines are strikingly beautiful and give the impression that they were put together by superb artists who loved what they were doing and did it with infinite skill, patience, and care. Typography, paper quality, selection of photographs, the stories printed, and the overall editing, speak of the publishing art brought to a peak of excellence. There are times when skimming through those pages that you believe the movies were created in order to be rediscovered in a fan magazine.

Modern Screen Magazine was introduced in 1930 with about two hundred pages containing dozens of striking studio portraits of movie performers, along with many scenes from movies, and casual on-stage or at-home photographs. The magazine carried about one hundred excellent pictures in an average issue. In addition, there was at least one *novelization*, that is, a specially created story based on a moving picture. The novelization was richly illustrated by carefully selected photos from the movie. There were factual and probably invented stories about the stars, producers, directors, costume designers, and writers. There were both factual and fictitious articles about how production companies overcame seemingly insuperable obstacles in making a movie. Oddities, intimate glimpses into personal lives, and accounts of "rags to riches" success filled the book-length magazine. In the year 1930 (only a relatively short time after the appearance of feature-length movies and a time when sound movies were only three years old), there were nostalgic articles looking back with immense pleasure to the "earlier" days of movie making.

Volume 1, number 6 of *Modern Screen*, published May 6, 1931, is a fanzine work of art. It would occupy a unique place in any collection. The softly hand-tinted cover is filled with a marvelous portrait of the lovely Marlene Dietrich. Miss Dietrich was then only twenty-seven years old and known mainly for her notable performances in the tremendously successful movie "The Blue Angel," made the year before. How could anybody have foretold that she would become one of filmdom's immortal stars? The glowing cover of the young star is a prophecy that the movie would be delighting audiences throughout the world continuously for the next half century. Tens of millions of people have been touched by this story of an ageing schoolteacher who is hopelessly and destructively in love with a sleazy night club singer. The massive but sensitive character actor Emil Jannings played the desperate school teacher and Marlene played the singer. No one who has seen the movie can forget her lithe movements or the song that has become her personal trademark, "Falling in Love Again."

The extraordinary May 6th issue continues with nostalgic articles about Rudolph Valentino, who had died tragically only a few years earlier, and about the amazing "little tramp" Charlie Chaplin who was still a relatively young man in 1930 but had already become an international legend. This issue of the fanzine, like most of the others for that year and afterwards, always gives credit to Chaplin as one of the founders of the movie art and industry. May 6th, 1931, is also a remarkable collectible because it contains a feature story about Richard Dix who was then winding up twenty record-breaking years as a leading man—a record that few male stars have been able to match. His look and manner of warm-hearted toughness set a style that was widely imitated by the up-and-coming young actors of the time such as James Cagney, Pat O'Brien, Clark Gable, and William Gargan. It was also a style adopted by millions of young men who thought of the combination of toughness and gentleness as male ideals.

This issue also contained a large number of extremely interesting and clear half- and quarter-page black-and-white or sepia photographs of actors and actresses, all suitable for framing or inclusion in an album. One of the reasons why fanzines are so scarce is that just as soon as the buyer finished reading them, they were cut up for the fine photographs. The issue, like many other fanzines of the period, included a biographical directory of the stars. Writing letters to the stars was encouraged and they were sure to be answered. The answer was signed by the star even though it was most often written by a writer in the publicity department, while the envelope that brought the answer usually contained a signed photograph and, on occasion, some other personal souvenir.

One of the wonderful aspects of the fanzines was the fact that they encouraged the reader to believe that he or she was participating in giving purpose and scope to the movies. Readers were encouraged to take part in writing contests by sending ideas to the screenplay departments of the studios and by sending letters to producers to let them know what they liked or didn't like in recent movies and what or who they wanted to see more of. The fanzines also encouraged readers to consider movie acting as a career, and there can be no doubt that the thousands of young people who headed to Hollywood each year with their hearts filled with dreams of stardom were encouraged by the fanzines.

The oldest fanzines are not the most interesting, beautiful, or valuable among all the fan magazines published. The oldest fanzine, *Photoplay Magazine*, which began in 1909, and its earliest competitor, *Picture Play Magazine*, which began in 1910, are, of course, extremely interesting and important to movie historians. They are also very valuable as pioneer ventures that developed the format and content which were copied by nearly every fanzine that followed. However, the actors and actresses, the directors and producing companies, the faces, the stories, and even the snippets of gossip seem very far removed from our own experience, and they are not striking enough by themselves or evocative enough of the movies they tell about to be important for memorabilia collectors. Their price is high because historically oriented collectors such as libraries, performing arts centers, and museums need to have complete historical collections, but these magazines are not the kind that you want to look at time and time again or show to your friends. The performers were none that we ever saw in the neighborhood movie house where we grew up or on television festivals of the old silents.

In 1940, fanzines were hit with sudden increases in production costs and paper shortages because of the war in Europe, which soon spread throughout the world. As a result, the size of each issue was reduced severely, and paper quality was such that it yellowed in the sunlight on the way home from the newspaper and magazine stand. There suddenly seemed to be very little interest on the part of the publishers in the photographic quality of the magazine or the editorial quality of the articles and stories. Fanzines after 1940 are bedraggled imitators of the beautiful issues that were so lovingly produced in the 1920s and 1930s. After 1940, they are just not the same from any standpoint, and there is very little interest in them for collecting purposes. In addition, and partly because of declining quality, there was a general falling off of interest in fanzines. In 1975, sales of fanzines dropped 25 percent to 35 percent from 1974 sales. A *Movie Mirror* of 1976 is a far cry from a 1930 *Silver Screen,* and it's easy to understand why collectors are willing to pay premium prices for the older and more beautiful issues.

The last of the high-quality collectible fanzines is *Screen Album Magazine.* This was mainly a photo album that appeared annually during the 1940s. It contained upwards of two hundred full-page portraits of the stars. Even though the paper was not of the best quality, the process for printing photographs was better than it had ever been and the portraits are remarkably interesting and worth owning. By 1942, most of the stars, who will be remembered with affection for as long as people have a chance to see their movies, had achieved fame and were in the prime of life. The *Screen Album* portraits show this quality of vitality and success and a youth that never seems to fade.

The best action scenes from the movies will not be found on the pages of the fanzines; since they had to be reduced in size to illustrate articles, stories, or novelizations, they are less interesting than the posed studio shots or portraits. Collectors interested in action scenes will not find much that is collectible in the fanzines.

Memorabilia collectors who are also fascinated by fashion trends will find a gold mine of valuable material in the fanzines. Each issue of nearly every magazine featured an interview with two or more stars who discussed the latest clothing designs, textiles, accessories, and ensembles— some of which they planned on using in their private lives and nearly all of which they would surely use in an upcoming movie. The French clothing designer, Chanel, was a favorite of many stars like Norma Talmadge and Gloria Swanson, both of whom enjoyed amazingly popular careers and who were among the many stars who set the fashion trends for millions of women. The richness of fashion design in the movies is available for enjoyment at a leisurely pace in the fanzines: what Marie Prevost thought of the latest design created for her (a black satin crepe gown), how Mae Busch thought she would feel in her next movie wearing a genuine ermine coatee (the kind worn mainly by royalty attending a Coronation), or the excitement felt by Gloria Swanson about to go to a formal party in an all-lace evening cape.

One of the best collectibles among the fanzines for those interested in the feature-length silent movies of the 1920s is *Screenland*. Its many issues during the golden decade of the silents are filled with colorful and entertaining information about the movies. In addition, each issue contains eighty or more exquisite full page 7″ x 9″ photographs suitable for framing. During this amazing movie era, celebrities were referred to as "famous film folk" or "celluloid luminaries" rather than as "stars" and "superstars."

Screenland contains affectionate articles and stories about people whose contributions to movie making are now the subject of long analytical books and studies but who, at the time, were seen mainly as ordinary people with a tremendous gift for entertaining others. One of the issues contains a rare, extremely informative, and beautifully illustrated story about Victor Seastrom. In the 1920s, Seastrom was Sweden's leading movie director and was invited to Hollywood, London, Paris, and Rome to inspire young directors and performers with his technical virtuosity and amazing ability to bring out the finest qualities of every actor and actress who appeared before his camera. Seastrom's towering personality and reputation had a powerful effect on movie making the world over, although most of his films are now forgotten and ignored. During the peak of his directing career he was referred to as "a great mastermind" and "a brooding genius of the film." These qualities were passed on to Ingmar Bergman, who revered the once great director and who imitated many of the "mastermind's" outstandingly successful techniques. As a tribute to his mentor, Bergman starred Seastrom, who was then over eighty, in an acting role in his remarkable movie about growing old, "Wild Strawberries" (1957).

One of the pleasures that fan magazine collectors can enjoy over and over again are the many well written stories about and unfamiliar photographs of actors and actresses in their first silent movie appearances after which they went on to achieve great fame in sound movies. For example, Boris Karloff is known to hundreds of millions for the roles he created in the early sound movies, roles that were mainly in horror stories. His most famous horror role is the classic monster he played in "Frankenstein" (1931). The fan magazines of the 1920s, though, show the wonderful British actor in a wide range of acting situations—including a New York City gangster and a kindly, sympathetic small-town father.

Among the most valuable fan magazines of the 1930s are the annual editions published by each of the monthly fan magazines. Each annual imitated the style of the others so that there are not many differences among them. They were luxury items then, although they cost only ten cents, and they are thoroughly enjoyable and valuable luxuries today. The inside dimensions were usually 7" x 9" and each page contained one or two gold-tinted studio portraits of the actors and actresses whom the editors of the fan magazines thought were among the most popular performers of the year. Their judgments seem amazing, almost prophetic, when you consider that so many of the performers who appeared on the lush pages of the annuals were in many cases only beginning their careers but later went on to become stars and held onto their popularity for years. Forty years has not diminished the appeal of such talents as Clark Gable, Greta Garbo, Mae West, Ginger Rogers, Fred Astaire, Katharine Hepburn, Claudette Colbert, James Cagney, Bing Crosby, Cary Grant, Marlene Dietrich, and Helen Hayes, among many others. Separately, a fine, tinted studio portrait of a star costs $5 to $7, but the annuals have 50 to 60 pages of excellent portraits. No wonder the price of an early 1930s annual in mint condition is between $200 and $300.

One quality of the old fan magazines that has consistently strong appeal to collectors is the delicately colored cover photographs printed in a costly, subtle two-color process that is no longer used. These gorgeous covers provide a vision of movie personalities and the movies themselves filtered by soft, loving tones. They are quite different from anything we have seen since the 1940s when covers became garish, blurred, and very much lacking in individuality. Today's covers are hard, excessively "loud" in their glaring colors, and without much visual connection with a particular movie or style of movie. The best of the soft-color covers are found on *Photoplay* and *Picture Play* magazines, and among the finest, earliest covers is "Little Mary Pickford." Of course, the Pickford name is synonymous with movies, and the first fan magazine glimpses, real or imagined, into her private life stirred up a fervor of literary activity which still continues over sixty years after it began— the Hollywood gossip column. Collectors should be warned that many of the fine old fan magazines that are still available, though not in mint condition, have had pages cut from them. These pages are usually the gossip stories, because over the years some collectors have saved only the gossip in the belief that there was very little else in the fan magazine worth reading or collecting. However, the entire magazine is beautiful and collectible—not just the gossip column or the marvelous cover.

Early *Photoplay* and *Picture Play* magazines provided their readers
with large amounts of information about the private lives of the movie
personalities. The stories of fame, success, riches, power, and high living
contained elements of sadness with forthright descriptions of excessive
drinking, gambling, promiscuity, divorce, sudden illness, and death. The
stories of the stars' personal lives echoed the risks and misfortunes of
everybody's life and, more important, the stories echoed the style of
most movies: clear cut differences between good and bad, between what
is moral and what is immoral, and between happiness and misery. "Celluloid personalities" were given reality by the fan magazines, and the
fan magazines made them even more important in the lives of the movie-
goers. The stars' losses became our losses, their misfortunes became our
own, and when "bad streaks" in their character served to deprive them
of health, wealth, or happiness, we could be reassured that somehow
there would always be justice. By the mid-1930s, the major fan magazines could each count over a million subscribers. This was a phenomenal number then, as it is now.

One of the most important parts of the best fan magazines of the
1920s and 1930s is the novelizations. Novelizations increase the value
of a fan magazine two to three times, depending on the quality of the
writing. And what novelizations they were! Nearly all novelizations were
stories written to be published *after* a movie was made. Most novelization writers were anonymous, but some were well known at the time,
such as Faith Baldwin, John O'Hara, and Sherwood Anderson. They
looked at the movie before writing—sometimes. Most often, they composed the novelization without a script or outline, with merely a discussion with the movie's director to learn what the story was about. After
they finished the novelization, editors and illustrators went to work providing stills from the still-unfinished movie. The end result was an exciting, illustrated, highly polished book-length story that cost ten cents in
most fan magazines and twenty-five cents in the others. Since the late
1950s, novelizations have appeared in book form, and the inexpensive
paperback editions are sold in the millions of copies since they usually
appear on the stands during the week in which the movie on which they
are based opens. Some book-form novelizations are as successful and
profitable as the movie itself—for example, the novelization of "Love
Story" by Erich Segal, based on the script he wrote for the movie. Some
novelizations are based on movies that were based on novels! The novelization, however, is very different from the original novel. For collectors,

it is the novelization that is the valuable memorabilia object and not the novel. For example, Nathaniel Hawthorne's novel *The Scarlet Letter* was made into a fine movie and a novelization of the movie appeared in a 1920s fan magazine. More people have probably read the novelization than ever read the original novel. The novelization was richly illustrated with carefully selected scenes from the movie. This was in 1913, and although people's tastes have changed so much since then, the novelization based on the movie "The Scarlet Letter" is still wonderfully readable and entertaining.

By modern printing standards, the fan magazines of the 1920s and 1930s were extremely limited in their use of color. Magazines that used varied colors had to use special paper and special printing presses just like the art books of the time. The cost of making such a magazine was high and a buyer had to spend a few dollars for each copy. A mass magazine designed to sell for ten cents could not use these costly methods. The magazines found a way around the problem—an ingenious way. They gave their readers a sense of vivid color by printing each issue with a different colored ink. One of the best collectibles that made use of special inks is *Screenplay Secrets*. One issue is printed entirely in deep blue ink, including the full-page photographic portraits and action scenes illustrating the novelizations and articles. The next issue is printed entirely in green, and another is printed in brown. Even the issues printed in varying shades of red ink give a sense of soft, subtle color that is enjoyable to look at, leaving much to the imagination without any of the harshness or the uneven, blurry quality of today's fan magazines. There is an expanding market of collectors ready to pay as much as forty dollars for a used but fine condition issue of *Screenplay Secrets* published between 1923 and 1927. While these issues are delightful and a worthwhile addition to any movie memorabilia collection, they are not quite as attractive or yet as valuable as other fanzines published between 1929 and 1935. Even if you don't agree that 1929 to 1935 was the "golden age of the movies," you cannot help agreeing that these years are the golden age of movie fan magazines.

Prices for Fan Magazines, 1919–1930

Here is a list of the most important fan magazine collectibles that appeared in the United States from their initial date of publication until the quality of fan magazines began to seriously decline beginning in

THE Universal Weekly

DEVOTED TO MOTION PICTURES

Vol. 1   Nov. 9, 1912   No. 21

JANE FEARNLEY
Latest Portrait of the Universal (Imp) Star

FAN
MAGAZINES

Collection: "Silver Screen"

Lonely? Join Rosemary Lee's Helping Hearts Club

MOVING PICTURE
STORIES

t 7, 1930
l. 37, No. 855

10¢

Sue
Carol

The LATEST ROMANCES *from the* SCREEN

FIRST, FOREMOST AND FINEST

Motion.Picture.

MARCH

MAGAZINE
20 CTS

ANETHA GETWELL

THE DEBT

RELEASED NOV. 21ST

TWO REEL REX

Her Honor at Stake

Paul Sacrifices Himself

The Love of Years Realized

The Wages of Sin

A most sublime story depicting the innocence of a southern lass, the treachery and cowardice of one man and the loyalty and bravery of another.

Portrayed with Dramatic Realism.

Artistically Staged. Photographically Beautiful.

A Rex feature that will live in your mind forever.

Universal Film Mfg. Co.

Mecca Building, Broadway at 48th St., New York City

During the filming of Old English, George Arliss and Leon Janney became great pals. The star's delight was to find some new mechanical toy to take to the Warner Brothers' Studio for the youngster. And Leon's delight, next to receiving the toy, was to proffer a licorice in return, then mischievously tuck it into the side of his mouth and slip off with the grin that is endearing him to the picture public.

That's That

By RUTH RAND

IS THERE money in the movies? Verily—unless Dame Rumor has lost all respect for the truth, for she has it that there is a hundred grand waiting to be collected by the fortunate person who can write an acceptable story for the lovely Billie Dove. Howard Hughes, young many-times-a-millionaire producer of "Hell's Angels", which, by the way, is running simultaneously at two Broadway houses and, it is said, may open at a third, is reported to be offering that amount. If only one could write that story—and then see the world, not through a port hole, either. And you never can tell who'll hit the target. For instance, there's Jane Hinton, a twenty-one-year-old college girl, who has sold her first story, "The Devil Was Sick," to First National. Well, that's enough to write any little devil's good, or otherwise, get well in double-quick time. When the story reaches the screen, it may be, "The Dark Angel Is Indisposed". But who cares?

Often looked about for the most contented place to carry your beauty when you haven't anything to put on your face? Mary Doran has discovered it. An extra hand around the hat and, presto, you have a traveling dress store! Wonder why she bought—and here's a thought of that. But maybe they have!

WHERE—not how—to live was the problem that confronted the Cedric Gibbonses (Dolores Del Rio and her husband) when they returned from their honeymoon. Dolores owns two houses and Cedric one—and is building a second, a wide sweeping Spanish palazzo in Santa Monica, which ought to be an ideal setting for the lovely, dark-eyed star from Mexico. They finally decided to establish their residence, for the present, at least, in Cedric's new shack, in which a special wing will house the bride's valuable collection of antiques. Well, anyway, here's one worry the rest of us are spared.

* * *

MARRIAGES of all professional folks are not just for a day. Take the Gleasons, Jimmy and his popular wife, Lucille. They recently celebrated their twenty-fourth wedding anniversary with a party at their Beverly Hills home. My, but the movies are getting old-fashioned! Pretty soon the boy-friend will be asking the girl-friend's father before he elopes with her.

* * *

REMEMBER the days when you couldn't wait for the next week to come around to find out if the hero rescued Pearl White from the burning building or knocked out the leader of the gang and cut the ropes and removed the gag that rendered the beautiful heroine helpless—and silent! Well, before long you'll have a chance to wait just as anxiously for the next week to come around, for Pathé is starting work on "The New Perils of Pauline" and "The New Exploits of Elaine". The original "perils" and "exploits" were released way back in 1914 and, of course, both perils and exploits undergo changes in sixteen years, so they don't "go native", they are pretty sure to "go modern". It will be interesting to see what new tricks they are up to now.

* * *

THE late Rudolph Valentino put the word "sheik" into the English language. Roland West is now considering remaking that popular picture as a talkie with Chester Morris in the rôle portrayed by the late

popular star. This will give the producer a splendid opportunity to check up on our friend Shakespeare when he said, "The play's the thing." And what an opportunity for a small house to show the silent version while the talking is in progress around the corner at the more pretentious house. Well, Roland West proved himself a first-class picker when he placed his faith in Chester Morris. That boy's good and his popularity is increasing with every mail—yes, and female, too—and especially.

* * *

WHEN "Hell's Angels" opened, one heard several murmurs in the audience, among them, "Who is she?" "Where did she come from?" "She's strong on looks." The *she* referred to was, of course, the girl. No one had seen or heard—and few had ever heard of her. It was just another of those "glass slipper" stories that keep hope burning in the hearts of young America's beautiful youth. The picture, as you probably know—perhaps you have heard your grandmother mention the fact—was started many moons ago. Then the talkies swept the cinema world upside down and producer Howard Hughes decided to scrap his silent angels and buy some talking ones, instead. Angels come high, but what are a few hundred thousands to a man whose income reads not like a telephone number but like the whole telephone book? Greta Nissen had the lead at that time, but though that particular blond-haired little beauty may be an angel, she fell from that part of the blue heaven reserved for the Scandinavian contingent—and that would never do. Then began the search for a blond angel minus an accent. Scores of tests were made and scores of voices tried.

Then one day, the hero, Ben Lyon, happened to be wandering over the Christie lot—we don't know where Bebe was at that time—and he spied an extra pretty extra girl. Still no Bebe! He learned that her name was Jean Harlow. He told his big boss about her, a test was made and Jean landed the part—her first important one.

The new find is variously reported to have come to California from both

Perhaps you have seen a lovelier picture of youth and its dream. We haven't. These faces look almost too idealistic to be real. But they are. They belong to Lucille Powers and Phillip Holmes, the youthful lovers in "Barber John's Boy".

Chicago and Kansas City. You pays your money and you takes your choice. Anyway, what does it matter? The locale of the picture isn't laid in either place.

CANINE actors on the screen have just the same road to travel as human players.

Twelve years ago Buddy was a star among picture dogs. He made his own two-reel comedies and was famous the world over. Now he's old. And, just as human actors, when they get old, go from romantic leads to character rôles—so 'tis Buddy. Today he is playing "old man" parts in the "all-barkie" comedies at the Metro-Goldwyn-Mayer Studios. In the newest, "All Quiet on the K9 Front", he appears as the old mayor of a French village.

The lure of pictures is still strong in him, and he acts as eagerly as younger dogs, and, in fact, is fully as agile. His son, Buddy, Jr., in-
(Continued on page 28)

Ever wondered how to consume an artichoke according to Hoyle? Crane toothternly! Elliott Nugent, appearing with Greta Garbo in "Romance", demonstrates the delicate operation. It's a serious business, too, if we are to judge from the concentration on the face of the well-known stage family's offspring.

1940. Foreign fan magazines are not included mainly because they are generally quite inferior, from every standpoint, to American fan magazines from the same period. Prices given are for fine to good condition used magazines. Mint condition magazines are worth two to three times the price given; magazines in less than fine to good condition, such as those published after 1940, can be bought for from $3.50 to $7.50.

Fan Magazine	First Published	Price
Hollyleaves	1919	$175.00
Movie Mirror	1932	75.00
Modern Screen	1930	100.00
Movies	1937	40.00
Moving Picture Stories	1913	200.00
Motion Picture Stars	1928	150.00
Motion Picture Story	1911	200.00
Photoplay	1913	250.00
Photoplay Journal	1916	225.00
Photoplay World	1917	250.00
Picture Play	1916	165.00
Screen Album	1934	100.00
Screen Book Magazine	1937	35.00
Screenland	1923	120.00
Screenplay Secrets	1927	150.00
Screen Romances	1929	125.00
Silver Screen	1930	100.00
Story World	1930	75.00

CHAPTER SIX

Press Books

Like the movies themselves, press books are an art form that drew upon the talents of many different people with as many different and highly developed skills. Press books, especially from the 1920s and early 1930s when this unique art form was developing, make handsome and enviable additions to any collection of movie memorabilia. Many are beautiful to look at, touch, and display, and they are fantastically interesting in providing intimate glimpses into movie-making and the lives of the movie-makers. Press books are among the most difficult memorabilia to collect, and the effort expended to acquire a good example of one will be rewarded many times over.

The term *press book* came into popular use in the movie world only during the mid-1930s. Before then these precious and delightful *objets d'art* were called *dossiers* (the French word for folders) since the publicity and promotion information that was to go out to newspapers, magazines, and distributors was contained in an oversized folder. They were also called *campaign books* since all of the printed, graphic, and novelty material contained in the packet was made up of plans, suggestions, and often wildly imaginative ideas that the movie studio promotion and advertising department believed would help in the campaign to arouse interest in a movie so as to "drive" people from their home to the nearest box office.

Among those who produced and distributed the press books, the term most often used from 1910 until the mid-1930s was *ballybook*, or, simply *bally*. The word came from *ballyhoo*, referring to any kind of energetic promotion designed to attract audiences in connection with a public entertainment. And the bally sparkled with energy and inventiveness. To promote John Boles' movie of marital intrigue, "So This Is Marriage" (1925), the ballybook urged that movie managers engage a handsome man who resembled John Boles (there was no shortage since Boles was one of the most fabulously popular leading men of the 1920s and early 1930s) who would stroll along Main Street escorting a sad looking but pretty woman on each arm with a sign borne on their shoulders: "Can You Be Happy and Unfaithful?" The movie was a tremendus success and without doubt much of the success was produced by hundreds of men resembling John Boles strolling down hundreds of Main Streets with signs reading "Infidelity!" and "Who Is Destroying *This* Marriage?" The ballybook is filled with suggestions for signs, how to attract young women to wear them, and how long in advance the "stroll" should take place so that people would remember the name of the movie house and the day of the first showing.

The earliest press books made their appearance shortly after World War I, around 1920, in connection with promotion for the feature-length dramatic silent films that began to appear in greater numbers. These early press books were actually published in the size of daily newspapers but a heavier, somewhat glazed paper was used and the type size was two to three times larger than that used by most newspapers. Perhaps the only present-day trace of the first ballybooks that continues to be published is the annual, year-end edition of *Variety*, which began as a campaign book for the entertainment industry in general.

From 1920 to 1925, the press books were very serious in trying to get across the many different ways a movie might be promoted in a given locality and at the heart of all the suggestions was detailed information about *how* the movie was made and equally detailed information about *who* the key performers were in real life. Much if not all of the information was invented so as to provide tantalizing snippets of gossip and breathtaking adventure that newspapers and magazines might repeat in their columns so as to whet the appetites of the audience. Nowadays some of the old-time bally for a movie appears on television in the form of one- to three-minute documentaries showing the actual filming of a movie. Much *who* detail is brought out on nightly talk shows on which performers attempt to appear as modest, average people trying to achieve certain results with their art. Movie advertising and promotion now rely heavily on television so that few press books are produced any more. The few that are produced are mainly samples of ads to be placed in local newspapers directed at telling the reader where the movie is playing. More detailed accounts about *how* the movie was made appear, more and more, in book-length stories written by the director or producer. Complete details about *who* appear, more and more, in biographies and autobiographies of performers almost always written in collaboration with a professional writer.

From the beginning of the 1920s it was certain that feature-length movies were going to remain the mainstay of the industry. The public was going to want more movies and would go at least once a week, and it became necessary for the advertising and promotion departments to expand their activities. And, as the ballyhoo activities expanded, the size of the press books expanded. The average length of the first press books, when they resembled newspapers in format, was sixteen pages. By 1930 the press book for one movie was close to sixty-four pages, and by 1935 the campaign book was actually a box of materials weighing one to two pounds and containing written and graphic materials in great variety. However, fewer of the boxed materials were produced compared to the earlier versions of the press book. This was primarily because the movie industry had become organized into a close-knit monopoly tying together production and distribution with promotion and exhibition; the need for effective advertising and promotion materials remained but the need for large numbers of copies went down. As a result, press books for the period from 1930 to 1935 are far more rare and valuable than press books of the 1920s or even the few budding campaign papers that began to make their appearance even before World War I, when movie ballyhoo was called the *production book*.

Press books from the 1920s provide lists of the articles that had been manufactured which managers could rent or buy to promote a particular movie. The press book contains, in many instances, vivid descriptions and, sometimes, photographs of the items suggested. A popular promotion suggestion of the time was to rent an elephant, camel, or giraffe from a local menagerie and have the colorful beast parade through town carrying flags, banners, and bunting announcing that a new Fairbanks adventure was opening at the Palace on Thursday. Another popular suggestion urged that stacks of attractively printed handbills, or *heralds* as they were called, be placed conspicuously on hotel and restaurant counters announcing a movie's opening. What we now readily recognize as "trailers" or "coming attractions," consisting of very brief scenes shown a week or two before the opening of a new film, was presaged during the 1920s by a gorgeously made slide in black and white or hand tinted in color that was inserted into the projector before the feature. The slide contained a single dramatic scene, a snippet of suggestive dialogue in a caption, and the day the movie was to open.

Slides from this period are extremely rare and precious. Unfortunately, many of them were made on glass and were discarded after the film opened rather than run the risk of breakage in shipping them back to a distribution exchange.

Press books for the entire period from 1920 to 1935 contained glowing descriptions of promotional contents, crossword puzzles, games, and specially made housewares and garments that could easily tie in with the advertising message at places where people were likely to be and receive the message. The objects have become rare and enjoyable collectibles for movie memorabilia buffs. Puzzles, games, dishes, cutlery, hats, ties, suspenders, and handkerchiefs, once given away at no cost, have become important items—beautiful, nostalgic, and expensive—for collectors.

At some time nearly every carefully prepared detail that went into the composition of a movie scene was manufactured into an object or made available in some way to tie in with movie promotion and all are aptly identified in the pressbooks: buttons, cufflinks, sporting equipment, drinking glasses, "boudoir furnishings," and hairdos were among the hundreds of everyday things and impressions on the mind's eye that could be related to the movies. Toys and rugs were promoted "as you saw them" in such and such a film. This helped to sell box office tickets and it helped to promote the sale of merchandise for local businesses that displayed the items suggested in the campaign book. The excitement of being able to enjoy in real life the styles set in the movies became a pleasurable pursuit for many movie-goers. As soon as "The Thin Man" series, starring Myrna Loy and William Powell, became immensely popular with millions of Americans (1934 marked the first of a series of six), their pet Scottish Terrier started a national craze to own a lively little Scottie. Very few American men in their twenties did not own or wish very much to own the wide-brimmed, light-colored fedora made popular by a score of stars in the innumerable gangster movies of the early 1930s.

Press books were expensive to make. A lot of talent went into their production: gifted writers, layout artists, editors, photographers, highly imaginative "idea" people, printers, artists, and promoters. For very expensive movies perhaps fifty to one hundred press books were made; for low cost "A" or first feature movies only twenty to fifty—at most —were made. As a rule, "B" pictures did not have to be promoted and no press books were made for them; the main attraction was the thing that sold the tickets *plus* the idea that there was going to be a second feature-length movie. The second feature itself was not important enough to invest in costly press books. Because there were only six major production studios during the 1920s and early 1930s making expensive feature films, relatively few press books were made and they are now extremely scarce. In more ways than one they are equivalent to the limited, numbered editions of beautiful art books.

The monopoly that existed among the major companies during this period also extended to the manufacture and distribution of the tie-in items promoted in the press books. This can be seen in the press books of different companies which were each urging the use of the same kinds of items usually made by the same manufacturers.

Here are some of the kinds of things that are to be found in nearly every press book made before 1950—the year the major studios began to be dismantled and replaced by dozens of small, independent production companies and press books began to be replaced by other, newer forms of advertising and promotion:

—Excerpts from the contracts between the stars and the production studio. Audiences in the early days of the movies, as now, liked to know how much a star was being paid for each picture or a series of pictures or on an annual basis. From the details of a contract, magazines and newspapers which used the information to stir the public's imagination would almost always conclude that the budget for a movie would be high if the star's salary was high. Of course, most people thought an expensive picture would be better, for many reasons, than a less expensive film. (An original contract for a movie, "The Sheik" (1921), signed by Rudolph Valentino and the film's producer and mounted on a panel beside a sepia duo-tint portrait of that great romantic leading man was sold in 1975 for $7500.)

—A long, vivid, and absorbing synopsis of the story. As anyone who has ever been given a high school English assignment to write a summary, précis, or synopsis of a short story or novel will remember, it is short and to the point, usually about 200 to 300 words. Not so the press book synopsis. These were more nearly like short stories, 3000 to 5000 words long and beautifully written. They were not mere condensations or summaries—they were miniature literary gems on their own. The object of the synopsis was to generate enthusiasm in the newspaper or magazine writers to whom it was given with the intention of encouraging them to use the rich information in a newspaper or magazine story and thereby stir up audience interest. It mattered little that much of the synopsis detail was invented by the writer. There was enough material so that a reporter would be able to write the kind of summary that pleased him the most, and no two summaries appearing in the newspapers and magazines were alike. A full, rich, skillfully woven press book synopsis could furnish a range of choices for summarization in accordance with tastes in the northeast, the southwest, in big cities, and in small towns. Especially in the early days of the movies, what got audiences curious to know more was quite different along the Atlantic Coast than it was west of the Mississippi.

—Feature stories. These are beautifully crafted and skillfully written "non-fiction" stories about how the movie was made and about some of the movie's leading personalities: producer, director, actors, and "title writer" for the silents and "scenarist" for the sound movies. Some of America's most prestigious professional writers thought they would earn fame and fortune by creating movie scripts in Hollywood, but wound up in publicity departments assigned to write feature stories for press books. F. Scott Fitzgerald, John O'Hara, Nathaniel West, and many others produced hundreds of times more press book stories than scenarios. This helps to explain why these anonymous stories are so masterfully written. In many repects they are genuine works of the imagination, since the details they describe never happened: a director nearly falling from a cliff while attempting a bold angle shot; a mysterious stampede of wild beasts that nearly wrecked the camera equipment; sudden, unexplained illness and the absence of proper medical attention; in short, a rich fantasy of mishap to whet the audience's appetite and win attention for a movie. Many of the stories were written months before the shooting on a movie even began, so the writer did not have the benefit of a script or outline—only a conversation with a producer. As a result, the richly inventive feature story was often woven into the movie. Feature stories about the stars were almost always total inventions because earlier audiences, press book creators believed, wanted to believe that the lives of the stars off camera were as interesting and glamorous as in the movies. Many of the "facts" that appear in "official" biographies of the stars are embroidered repetitions of the inventions that appeared in press book feature stories.

—Women's fashion and beauty. An important section was found in all screen magazines and women's magazines describing how the stars solved their fashion questions, their make-up and coiffure questions, and their complexion problems. The fashion and beauty section was developed with a great deal of care and attention since the press book creators knew that millions of women would, if the movie became a smash hit, adopt the fashions used in the movie and change their hairdos and make-up to resemble the styles set by the movie's heroine. Because fashion was extremely important to the women's clothing industry, the press book urged exhibitors to tie their promotional activities in with local fashion shows, fashion reporting, and even clothing advertisements.

—Lovingly prepared biographies of every member of the cast. Lots of personal information—not human interest material but personal facts—was included so that an actress raised in Wichita Fails or Hoosick, no matter how small her role in the movie, might be singled out in a newspaper or magazine story by a writer who had some tie to one of those towns. These wonderful biographies reflect the tremendous appeal the movies had on people from all over the country who were drawn to Hollywood.

The balance of the press book is divided into two or more sections, depending on how much ballyhoo the studio wanted to put behind the movie. One section is devoted to scores of specific ideas about how to organize local promotional campaigns and details about particular things that might be done in the absence of a broad publicity campaign. Other sections—and these are of special interest to collectors—are lists of advertising and promotion "accessories" that could be bought, rented, or obtained free of charge to help promote the movie. All of these accessories are now valuable collectibles.

There seems to have been no limit to the imagination of the "idea" people who conceived the movie promotion campaign plans. In reading the old press books, you quickly get the impression that they had a perfectly marvelous time dreaming up the plans that were aimed at providing potential box office customers with "fun" things to do on their way to buy a ticket. Fan clubs were among the most popular ideas. There were fan clubs for particular stars, and fan club officers were given lots of help by the people in the studio promotion department who helped create the press books. Members received membership cards, buttons, insignia, banners, photographs, statuettes, certificates, and clippings, as well as newsletters and magazines. Some of the scrapbooks put together by devoted fans are priceless collectibles, and some collectors of scrapbooks originally assembled by fan club members have sold their entire collections to be preserved and exhibited at museums for prices well over $10,000.

There were also extremely popular fan clubs that promotion departments helped to organize around a particular kind of movie or a specific
movie. In the press book for "Northwest Passage" (1940), starring
Spencer Tracy, Robert Young, Walter Brennan, and Ruth Hussey, a
campaign plan is spelled out to set up a national network of Ranger
Clubs whose young members would be inspired by the spirit of adventure and courage exemplified by Rogers' Rangers, on whose exploits
the movie was based. Even before the movie opened hundreds of Ranger
Clubs had sprung up all over the United States. The purpose of the clubs
was to promote the love of the out-of-doors, protection of the wilderness,
protection of wildlife, and loyalty to fellow Rangers. Available to club
members were the following articles (now rare collectibles): kidskin or
buckskin fringed jackets, a floppy kind of coonskin cap that Spencer
Tracy wore in the movie, and membership emblems featuring artwork
about wild animals that inhabit North America.

Other pressbook promotion ideas included: theater parties, recep-
tions, discussion groups, fairs and picnics, and the press books provided
sample invitations for each and suggestions about movie related display items, which have become collectibles. Other tie-in promotions
suggested were displays of movie related books at local school libraries
and book stores, and displays in local department store windows (a
Cagney-style fedora might be shown in a shop window display of men's
clothes with a window card for a forthcoming movie starring James
Cagney).

The remaining portion of the press book was devoted to lists and
descriptions and photographs of accessories. In the earliest ballyhoo days
the most popular and colorful accessories were snipes, heralds, banners,
and burgees. The snipe was a printing block containing the name of a
movie house; all a theater manager had to do with an ad furnished
by the studios was to print his theater name and it was ready to be put
to use. Heralds, banners, and burgees are basically embossed, printed,
or embroidered pieces of glossy satin, fringed with gold and exotically
tasseled. When mounted on gold poles with finials or arrowheads they
fluttered from marquee or lobby ceilings as if to announce the arrival
of foreign royalty or fabled heroes and heroines from the pages of King
Arthur. Some of them were forty feet long, some only slender swallow
tails of eighteen inches to two feet, but all contained some unmistakable
fragment of a scene from the movie being promoted.

Two of the most elaborately ballyhoo'd movies of all times—at least

from the size and cost of the press books that were produced to promote them—are "A Virtuous Vamp" (1923), starring Constance Talmadge and, with one of the great press books of all time, "Our Little
Girl" (1935), starring Shirley Temple. Here is a sampling of the accessories that were listed in the press books—a treasure for any movie
memorabilia collector.

A Virtuous Vamp

2 types of 1-sheet poster
2 types of 3-sheet posters
1 6-sheet poster
1 24-sheet poster
1 rotogravure herald
set of 10 8″ x 10″ sepia lobby posters
set of 2 22″ x 28″ colored lobby cards
set of 8 lobby photos
set of 35 press stills
2 9½″ x 22″ color window cards
3 design slides
1 special music cue sheet—silents and piano
set of 5 star stills

Our Little Girl

20 8″ x 10″ black-and-white stills of scenes
20 autographed portraits of Shirley Temple
2 dolls in likeness of Shirley Temple
12 buttons
1 13″ x 16″ banner
sets of dresses and clothes
set of books and stationery
glass tumblers with decals
occasional dishes in glass
chinaware with Shirley Temple decal and motifs
soap novelties
hair ribbons
garters
booklets
picture puzzles and dialogue contests
auto tire covers
figurettes and life-sized standees

Press Book Bally Accessories—Prices Then and Now

Item	Original Price	Current Price
News ad mats of various widths and lines	none	$10.00
Streamers	$ .25	20.00
Banners, burgees, valences, snipes	1.00	50.00–100.00
Button 1½″ diameter	11.00 per 1000	2.00–10.00 each
Puzzles	.25	10.00–20.00
Caps, hats	.10	5.00–15.00
Novelty pens, lighters	.25	2.00–5.00
Bumper banners	.10	5.00–10.00
Blotters, book marks	.10 per 1000	2.00–5.00 each
Ties, garters, hosiery	.25 per item	10.00–20.00 per item
Perfume bottles, plain	.10	2.00–5.00
Perfume bottles, sculpted with likeness	.25	10.00–20.00

CHAPTER SEVEN

Movie Books: Novelizations, Big Little Books, Scrapbooks, and Books About the Movies

One sure sign of *liking* a movie was when you stayed in your seat to see it a second time. You can probably remember people saying, "I was crazy about that picture. I went twice last week to see it!" And if you *loved* it, there were times when you felt embarrassed to tell your friends that you had gone to see it three times. I remember conversations in which friends boasted that they had seen a particular Marx Brothers comedy five or more times in the course of a single week. There is no word to describe this kind of enjoyment of a movie. There are very few entertainments, apart from the movies, that furnish pleasure over and over again. When the price of admission to a movie was small, you could see it over and over and you wouldn't feel the pinch. However, even when you could afford to see a movie you loved again, it might not be playing in your neighborhood or in your city. Television re-releases of past movies make it possible to see old-time favorites, while movie clubs make it possible for members to choose favorites and then show them on rented equipment and rented reels, usually as 16mm copies. And, more and more, popular favorites are being made on 8mm and 16mm regular reels or on video cassettes so that they can be seen at home at any time by means of a projector or the home telvision set. For many, however, the pleasures of a particular movie are recalled not only by seeing the movie again but also by reading the story of the movie in a specially prepared version, often illustrated with choice stills taken from the movie. These versions are the *novelizations* that have long been a favorite of movie memorabilia collectors. Novelizations are book-length stories that try to faithfully put into print what is seen and heard in the movie house. A novelization is not the book, fiction or non-fiction, that

123

a movie may have been based on. It is an *original creation* based on the movie. Some collectors whose main interest is books have developed fine collections of books made into movies. The value of these books is negligible for memorabilia collectors—except when the publisher produced a special edition after the movie was released, and only when the special version contains graphic matter relating to the movie. Novelizations are far more valuable.

The first novelizations, referred to as such, were not book-length stories at all. They were rather like long short stories published in fan magazines and they were rarely made into book form until after 1920. In the chapter on fan magazines, you will find material on the novelizations that appear in fan magazines; here we are concerned with novelizations appearing as books. A good example is "Gone With the Wind." The novel written by Margaret Mitchell became an extremely popular best-seller in the late 1930s. The fabulous movie starring Clark Gable and Vivien Leigh was based on the novel. For memorabilia collectors the novel has little or no interest, even though twenty different editions of the book were published carrying dust jackets with scenes from the movie, and sometimes even black-and-white illustrations. However, several unauthorized novelizations have appeared which are much shorter than the original novel and which are based not on the book but entirely on the movie. These novelizations, especially the earliest editions, are very precious memorabilia. A very recent example of a popular novelization is the short one of "Love Story" which Erich Segal based on his original screenplay for the movie. Both the movie and the novelization were extremely popular. Every novelization collector probably has a copy of the "Love Story" book.

There are a few things to look for when deciding to acquire a novelization. First and foremost is good condition: solid binding, no yellowing pages, nothing torn from the book, no markings. Second, the story should read well, quickly giving a full, rich sense of the movie. Third, it should be illustrated with numerous black-and-white photographs (recent novelizations may include color) of scenes from the movie. These are basic values to look for. Other values include autographs of principals of the movie—the stars, director, producers, and sometimes, but rarely, the author. Most of the novelization authors used pen names because they felt that their reputations as "serious" writers would be hurt if word got around that they were writing books based on movies. A novelization published before 1950 and containing the author's autograph is highly likely to be a joke. Authors who wrote movie novelizations were paid very little for their effort even when the book became successful.

Among the oldest and rarest novelizations are those published during the 1920s, including "The Freshman," based on the Harold Lloyd movie. The novelization was very popular and though the original idea for the book was to provide people who had seen the movie with a way of continuing the experience, its popularity caused hundreds of thousands of people to see the film only *after* they had read the novelization. Another rare collector's item of the 1920s is the novelization of the Clara Bow movie "The Fleet's In." Recent novelizations which have won recognition by collectors include: "King of Kings," "El Cid," "Judgment at Nuremburg," and the novelization for the Jerry Lewis movie "Ladies' Man." Novelizations sometimes appear after a movie has been nominated for or has actually won an Academy Award. Among the outstanding collectibles in this category are: "Underworld," a novelization written by the well-known author Ben Hecht, who was among the few professional writers who was proud to put his name to a novelization; "Dawn Patrol," based on one of the great airplane adventures of all time; "The Champ"; "The Story of Louis Pasteur"; "Boy's Town"; and the ever-popular "Mr. Smith Goes to Washington."

Scenarios

Scenarios have always been a fascinating collectible among specialists. As more and more people become knowledgeable about movies and movie making, more and more people have become interested in collecting scenarios. Very recent scenarios representing all of the technical and artistic activity that entered into the making of a movie are extremely difficult to read and understand, and are collected by only a small number of specialists interested in the techniques of movie making. These are referred to as "final release scenarios" or scripts. They represent an edited gathering of all the different technical papers used in making the movie: cues, camera movements, set and costume decisions, location information, shooting time for each scene, notations for introduction of credits and music, and so forth. The importance of these scenarios will no doubt increase in the future as more people come to understand how to read and enjoy them. At present, they are like articles in a foreign language that you do not understand. Edited versions of these complicated scenarios appear in book format along with stills, logs of the director, the director's comments, interviews with some of the stars, and a synopsis of the story. Scenarios such as these have only recently come to be valued by collectors and then only by specialists in the artistic and technical achievements of certain directors.

Before 1920, hardly any scenarios were made at all. Directors usually worked from a handwritten outline or scraps of paper describing ideas they had for particular scenes. Since silent movies had no dialogue, there was no need for a script and most directors improvised a good deal in any case. Once in a while someone at the studio prepared a typewritten *outline* of the movie story and how the film was made; these are extremely rare notes but without much memorabilia value unless they contain the handwriting and signatures of people whose names are important to movie history.

The most interesting scenarios or scripts (the words are used interchangeably) for collectors are those made before, during, and after the making of a movie and mainly during the period from 1930 to 1950. These are usually typewritten or mimeographed, between 80 and 120 pages long, and bound in a soft leatherette or pasteboard binder. These are the scripts that were in the hands of the movie makers: actors learned their parts from these scripts, set and costume designers developed their plans from them, and directors worked from them or used them as a guide. They are very readable and some of them have notations by the people who used them, including their autographs. At the end of making a movie there is traditionally a party sponsored by the director, and at the parties those who made the movie often brought along their scripts, as souvenir albums, for everyone to sign. Such scenarios are extraordinarily valuable.

Books About the Movies

About 1,500 books have been published in English dealing with the movies. They range from very complicated discussions and essays about what a movie should be, to very amusing or sad biographies and autobiographies of movie makers. When I started a collection of books about the movies, I found that the quality of the books varied about as much as the topics, and that most people writing them were really writing about their ideas and not about the movies. Most of these books are fairly dull, and if you want to enjoy a movie more after seeing it the first time, it is better to see it a second or even a third time than to get a headache trying to understand why some authors think there is, say, a hidden political message in the use of the montage. The biographies and autobiographies, except for a few rare books, are badly written and either tell too much of the type of gossip that makes you wish you hadn't heard it or tell so little about the person that you want to rush to get your money back. The best books about the movies are those picture books that contain just enough written material telling about the movies and the people who made them. And the variety is enormous: from books about the movies of famed directors to books about bathtub scenes; from books bound in cheap paper selling for very little to books printed on luxurious paper with rich, glamorous photography costing a great deal. As a rule, books about movies are printed in relatively small quantities and are sold at discount prices within a year after they appear, so it is possible to amass a very select, high-quality collection without a heavy investment of time or money. A good library of books about movies will appreciate slowly in value as a library and not as individual books, unless they contain some unique element such as the autograph of the star who is the subject of the book, or if the book contains an unusual arrangement of rare photographs. Among the best features of collecting books about the movies is that you will have a good research library readily available for learning more about the movies and about other movie collectibles.

Scrapbooks

Over the years countless people have been informal collectors of movie memorabilia by keeping scrapbooks. However, scrapbook collecting usually lasts a short time, only a few years; afterwards, the scrapbooks find their way into the oblivion of a closet, attic, basement, or garage. However, some scrapbook collectors kept up their interest for many, many years and ended by selling or giving hundreds of volumes to a college, museum, or library. Many outstanding scrapbooks, individually and in scrapbook collections, have come into the possession of dealers, and are available to collectors. By careful prospecting, you may find scrapbooks to build an exquisite collection. The collectibles that are found inside scrapbooks are valuble in themselves and a lovingly assembled scrapbook is in itself a miniature collection.

Movement in
Two Dimensions
OLIVE COOK

MOVIE BOOKS

Collection: Cinemabilia

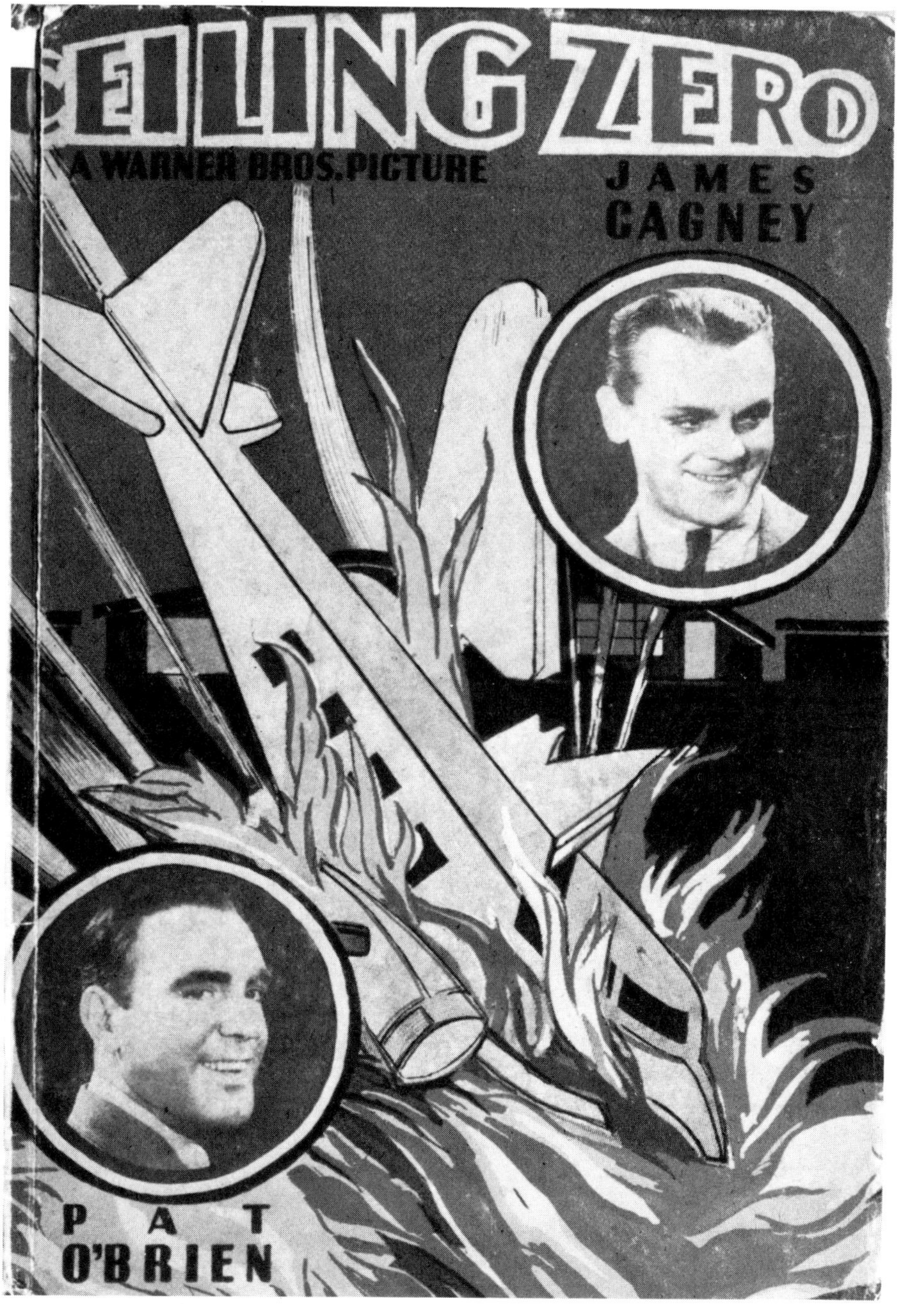
CEILING ZERO
A WARNER BROS. PICTURE
JAMES
CAGNEY
PAT
O'BRIEN

The JAZZ SINGER

Novelized by
ARLINE DE HAAS
FROM THE PLAY BY
SAMSON RAPHAELSON

Illustrated with
Scenes from the
Photoplay.....
A WARNER BROS.
PRODUCTION
Directed by...
ALAN CROSLAND

Starring AL JOLSON and MAY McAVOY

BEAU GESTE

P. C. WREN'S
Novel Illustrated
with scenes from the
Paramount Picture

RONALD COLMAN as 'Beau Geste'

WINGS

by JOHN MONK SAUNDERS

Based on the Paramount Picture ....
A Lucien Hubbard Production · Directed by William A. Wellman

DON Q'S
LOVE
STORY

BY K AND HESKETH
PRICHARD

This Novel
served as the
basis for
DOUGLAS
FAIRBANKS'
TREMENDOUSLY POPULAR
PHOTOPLAY
DON Q SON OF
ZORRO

ILLUSTRATED WITH SCENES FROM THE PICTURE

Illustrated with 43 photographs

Will acting spoil Marilyn Monroe?

BY PETE MARTIN

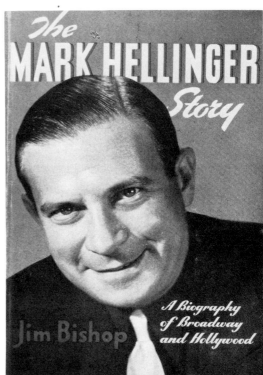

The MARK HELLINGER Story

Jim Bishop

A Biography of Broadway and Hollywood

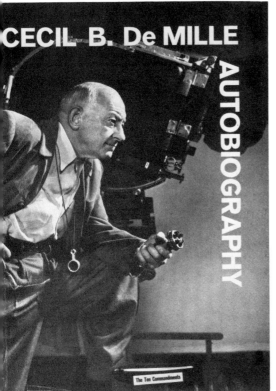

CECIL B. De MILLE

AUTOBIOGRAPHY

The Ten Commandments

The OLIVIERS

A Biography by FELIX BARKER

BUSINESS AND PLEASURE

PHOTOPLAY TITLE OF "THE PLUTOCRAT"

by BOOTH TARKINGTON

A FOX PHOTOPLAY
Starring
WILL ROGERS

G&D
GROSSET & DUNLAP

GENERAL CRACK

by GEORGE PREEDY

G&D
GROSSET & DUNLAP

Illustrated with scenes from the Warner Bros. All Vitaphone Production starring JOHN BARRYMORE

NANA

Complete and Unabridged

by EMILE ZOLA

ANNA STEN IN THE SAMUEL GOLDWYN PRODUCTION

a paramount picture

SHE DONE HIM WRONG

by Mae West

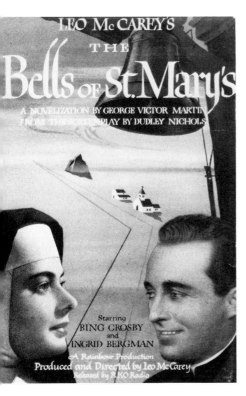

LEO McCAREY'S
THE
Bells of St. Mary's

A NOVELIZATION BY GEORGE VICTOR MARTIN
FROM THE SCREENPLAY BY DUDLEY NICHOLS

Starring
BING CROSBY
and
INGRID BERGMAN

A Rainbow Production
Produced and Directed by Leo McCarey
Released by RKO Radio

Duel in the Sun

The intensely dramatic novel of the American Southwest, from which the David O. Selznick technicolor film was made, starring JENNIFER JONES, GREGORY PECK & JOSEPH COTTEN. A Forum Motion Picture Edition.

Niven Busch

Spellbound

FRANCIS BEEDING

A story of madness and terror, from which the Alfred Hitchcock film was made, with Ingrid Bergman and Gregory Peck. (Formerly titled The House of Dr. Edwardes)
A Selznick International Picture released through United Artists.

A Forum Motion Picture Edition
KITTY

A romantic novel by
Rosamond Marshall

A story of
a London girl of the streets, from which the Paramount film was made, starring PAULETTE GODDARD and RAY MILLAND

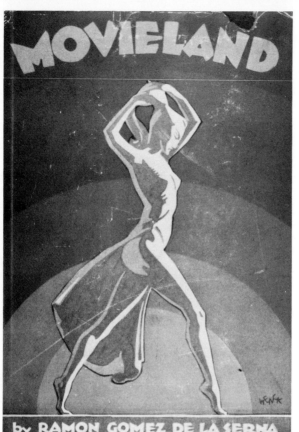

MOVIELAND

by RAMON GOMEZ DE LA SERNA

MONSIEUR BEAUCAIRE

A Paramount Picture

BY BOOTH TARKINGTON
RUDOLPH VALENTINO EDITION

The customary things that found their way into scrapbooks include:

—movie programs, sometimes souvenir programs of a premiere or souvenir program of a personal appearance by the movie's star. A souvenir program for a personal appearance by Bela Lugosi in a re-release of his celebrated "Dracula" (originally released in 1930) would normally cost $25, or $40 if he signed the black-and-white 8" x 10" glossy that was included in the souvenir program. The program will be worth much more if it is part of a well-assembled scrapbook on movies in general, on movies of the early thirties, on horror movies, or, most valuable of all, as part of a collection of "Dracula" movies.

—stills
—post cards
—blotters, flyers, club membership cards
—newspaper and magazine clippings
—other flat paper objects

Some scrapbooks contain letters to and from stars, and these are unique, particularly if they also contain other materials about the movie personalities who wrote the letters. Scrapbooks often contain novelization book jackets, reviews of the novelizations, and personal photographs taken with a star during a promotion tour.

The rarest and most costly scrapbooks are, of course, albums maintained by movie personalities themselves or by their close friends and relatives.

A typical scrapbook collection maintained by a movie personality can easily involve ten or more volumes, each running to about 50 pages. An average price for such a collection, say for an actor or actress enjoying popularity in the early 1930s, would be $100 per volume or $1000 for a collection of fewer than ten volumes. A typical scrapbook kept by a movie-goer during the same period is likely to consist of two fifty-page volumes containing about ten 8" x 10" glossy signed portraits of some personalities, about four autographed picture cards or signed letters, 15 to 20 newspaper ads and as many clippings, and probably a number of rarities like snipes, a lobby card, or insert. A movie-goer's scrapbook is more likely to cover the personal life of a star than the career of the star. Either type, however, brings considerable pleasure to collectors and good prices. A Wallace Beery scrapbook kept by a movie-goer brings $50 to $100 depending on the quality—and this is quite important, since no two collectors could possibly have developed identical scrapbooks on the same star. A Carole Lombard scrapbook sells for between $75 and $125, and the handsome scrapbooks maintained on Leslie Howard command $150 or more. Scrapbooks on movie themes, such as westerns, spy films, war movies, love stories, and the like, are generally less expensive.

Big Little Books

Big Little Books and their first cousins, the ever entertaining Flip Books, are important collectibles which appeared in book format from the very earliest days of the movies. They have pleased people of all ages for the sixty years since the first was produced.

Big Little Books are actually small-scale versions of movie novelizations, with reduced photographs and often line drawings that copy photo scenes from the movies. They range in size from 1″ x 1½″ to 3″ x 4″ and they are between 60 and 100 pages long. For millions of movie-goers in the late 1920s and early 1930s, movie-goers who had been in the United States for only a few years after immigrating from Europe, the Big Little Books were the most attractive way of building a vocabulary. The simple phrases used and the accompanying photographs helped these not very literate movie-goers to master the language. The books are not printed on very good paper and the bindings are often nothing more than thin pasteboard. However, when the nation's economy was badly hit in the 1930s, Big Little Books that cost a nickel or a dime provided millions of people with inexpensive entertainment that brought the movies into their homes. The Big Little Books are gems of style, miniature works of art, and vastly pleasurable memorabilia.

The Flip Book, BLB's little cousin, is actually the oldest form of moving picture entertainment. Like animation, the book consists of about fifty photographs showing different positions of a simple action, so that when you flipped them with your thumb you had the impression of a very brief movie. When Flip Books were installed in a machine and illuminated from inside by soft light, usually using between 200 and 300 photographs, the impression was far more complete and dramatic. Unfortunately, the price of one peek through the ancient "movie-ola" was anywhere from a penny to a nickel and you couldn't take it home, but you could keep the Flip Book. It rarely cost more than a penny, and was often given away by merchants as a premium. The price of Flip Books now ranges from two to ten dollars. The price range of Big Little Books is from five to twenty dollars.

CHAPTER EIGHT

Sound Tracks
and Other Movie Music

The great period of movie music began with the world's first sound movie, "The Jazz Singer," made in 1927 and featuring Al Jolson, then vaudeville's most popular singer. "The Jazz Singer" had only a few patches of conversation but contained lots of songs that were already popular in music halls throughout the country. Songs that were loved by hundreds of thousands of people would soon be on the lips of tens of millions and would become an important part of growing up in America. Although fifty years have gone by, the songs that "The Jazz Singer" brought into thousands of movie houses have become an important part of the artistic and musical heritage of America. Almost everyone's heart strings are tugged a bit by "Sidewalks of New York," "My Gal Sal," "In the Good Old Summertime," "My Mammy," "Blue Skies," and "Toot, Toot, Tootsie, Goodbye."

There was movie music before 1927, but it is more of an oddity than genuine movie memorabilia. For about twenty years before sound movies became a reality, music publishing companies as well as movie production companies distributed sheet music to the pianists or organists who played background music during the showing of silent movies. Composers were rarely, if at all, asked to create music for a particular silent film. Background organ and piano sheet music was usually made up of repetitious musical phrases that could be used for many different films. In the last few years some recording companies have made records based on sheet music from the silent period and while the recordings, like the old sheets, are interesting there is no important collector demand for them.

Although nearly all movies made since 1941 contain original music for serious dramatic, comedy, or musical films, a lot of it memora-

137

My One And Only Highland Fling

Lyric by IRA GERSHWIN   Music by HARRY WARREN

FRED GINGER
ASTAIRE ROGERS
in THE
BARKLEYS
OF
BROADWAY

with OSCAR LEVANT
BILLIE   GALE   JACQUES
BURKE   ROBBINS   FRANCOIS
Original Screen Play by BETTY COMDEN and ADOLPH GREEN
Music by HARRY WARREN   Lyrics by IRA GERSHWIN
Musical Numbers Directed by ROBERT ALTON
Directed by CHARLES WALTERS
Produced by ARTHUR FREED
A METRO-GOLDWYN-MAYER PICTURE

Harry Warren MUSIC, IN
NEW YORK 19, N. Y.
By arrangement with CHAPPELL & Co., Inc.

ble, moving, and beautiful, the most important collector's items are sound tracks covering the period from 1927 until 1941. There are numerous reasons why the earlier soundtracks are more valuable to memorabilia collectors, but a prominent one is that the earlier music was composed with a particular movie in mind. There was hardly a thought that people would be interested in buying a record of a theme or a musical sketch in the way they would buy a record of a well-known singer performing songs already popular through the opera, music hall, or radio. Although the "Raindrops Keep Fallin' " song from the movie "Butch Cassidy and the Sundance Kid" is a wonderful, singable, memorable song, its popularity depends mainly on its musical quality and less on its ability to bring to mind the action or performances in the movie or the particular scene in which the song was featured. This is very different from "Somewhere Over the Rainbow" from the "Wizard of Oz," starring Judy Garland. That song is hard to separate from the touching, poignant scenes in which Judy Garland sings it, and humming only a few bars of the melody conjures up images of the entire movie.

Since 1965, movie music has become increasingly important for collectors, and many different kinds of records of many different quality levels have appeared on the market. The great variety of recordings affects values for collectors and collections. It is therefore important to know some of the terms used and facts about movie music recordings in order to know what to get and to know what you're getting.

Between 1927 and 1941, roughly, the musical part of a movie was added to the sound track after the movie had been made and edited. In special sound studios, a *playback disk* or *playback record* was made containing all the music of any kind which was being considered for use in the movie for which it was composed or played. The best sound for the complete movie was on the playback disk. When the movie opened, the sound that the audience heard was on a magnetic track onto which it had been transferred from the original disk. What are called *original sound track* recordings for the period from 1927 to 1941 do not refer necessarily to the better sound quality records made from the playback disks but probably refer to a recording, of lesser sound quality, made directly from the magnetic track sealed onto the film itself. For collectors, the difference is substantial both in terms of sound quality, authenticity, and cost.

There are also substantial differences in *original pressings* as opposed to copies made from originals. Also, as with 8″ x 10″ stills, there are copies of copies and duplicates of duplicates. In the record industry, it is a fairly common practice for a major record producer who finds that it is no longer profitable to continue a particular title to drop the title from the list. However, because there is still some demand which may prove profitable for a smaller company, the smaller company will press a copy. This will probably be satisfactory from a sound quality stand-point but will not contain enough information for the collector to make a judgment as to its authenticity as a collectible that will increase in value over time. A record of Jeannette MacDonald and Nelson Eddy singing "Rose Marie" from the movie "Rose Marie" (1936) made from the first playback disk is worth twice as much as a record made from an original pressing taken from the movie sound track, and about ten to fifteen times more than a reissue of a copy made from an original pressing. If you are mainly interested in the quality of the sound, almost any recording that has a good sound to your ear is worth collecting because modern sound recording technology is able to blot out poor sound quality and actually improve musical values.

How many sound tracks are there altogether that are worth collecting? Before this question can be answered, you should know that the term "sound track" is often confused with a recording containing music or songs from a movie—but there are important differences. From the very beginning of sound movies some of the music and songs used in certain movies was recorded in regular record company studios. Special musical arrangements were made for such recordings and special studio orchestras were employed to play the music. However, if compared with what you could hear in a theater when the movie was shown, the *recorded version* would be very different. The *sound track* version was meant to be heard with the showing of the film and was actually heard in the first-run performances. (Pirated, bootleg recordings are often made by unscrupulous dealers from the sound tracks of films that have been repeatedly cut over the years to reduce running time or to keep a damaged print in circulation; the sound is so bad in these versions that most careful collectors can spot them immediately and refuse to buy them.) If you don't count recordings of music and songs made separately and only count sound tracks, there are probably only about 2,000 made from 1927 to 1941. About 800 of these were made from second features and "B" pictures whose musical values have generally been looked down on by musicians and are therefore not very well known to collectors. Another 500 to 600 sound tracks made use of music and song only incidentally as background for the opening titles and credits, for the closing scene, and during dramatic or special scenes at various points in the movie. These sound tracks, too, have unfortunately been frowned upon and are either not know to collectors or are not generally available. Of the remaining sound tracks, only about two to three hundred have been made into records—records that are becoming scarcer and rarer and more expensive with each year. A complete collection of movie music sound tracks from 1927 to 1977 would involve about 1000 records.

Because original pressings from the great period are becoming harder to find and because costs are skyrocketing, the collector should be prepared to accept one of several studio-made arrangements of music and song based on a sound track or the movie score for the music. Among the rare records of this period, for example, is the sound track for the 1936 movie "Roberta." The fabulous song, "The Way You Look Tonight," is virtually impossible to find on the original pressing, but there are at least 15 different arrangements that have been recorded since 1936 with as many different vocalists and each is a delight that almost does the job of evoking this wonderful movie.

According to Bruce Lisanti, a tremendously knowledgeable collector of movie and show records who is in charge of this department in one of the world's largest record shops (Bruce has over 2000 rare movie and show records in his collection), a collector of movie sound tracks should emphasize *either* the musical qualities in his collection *or* the profit value, and both require an investment of time. One of the things that will help record collectors is the knowledge that 45rpm, 33rpm, and cassettes came into being only after 1945, and that all the records of the great period are available exclusively on 78rpm disks. Re-issues of the original 78rpm pressings on 45rpm, 33rpm, or cassettes are likely to be very recent or were made from old sound tracks but not from the original playback disk. However, in cases where they know that some sound tracks are going to be appreciated for a long time, record companies have made an effort to maintain high standards of quality while keeping prices, at least for a while, at reasonable levels.

Beginning sound track collectors, to become familiar with record dealers and collectors, should start with a modest collection representing the six different musical areas: the musical landmarks, composers and songwriters, personalities (singers), themes and songs, and entire films. Once you become familiar with the musical and dollar values in each

SHEET MUSIC

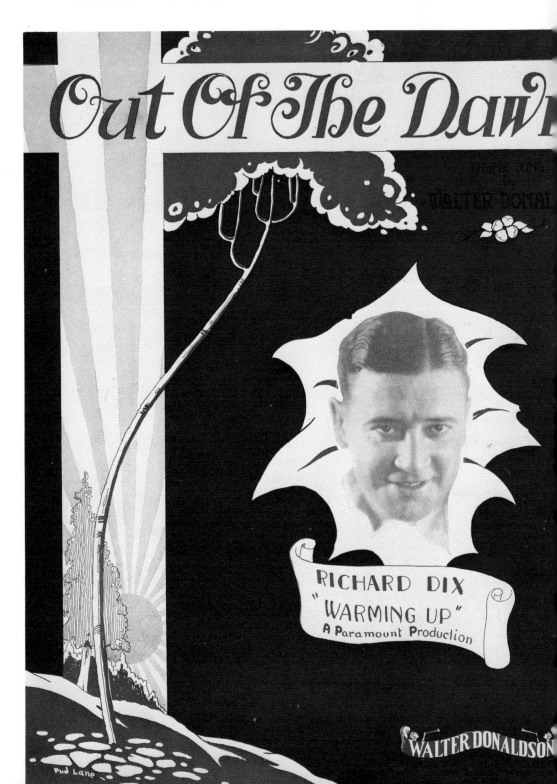

SOUNDTRACKS

Collection: House of Oldies

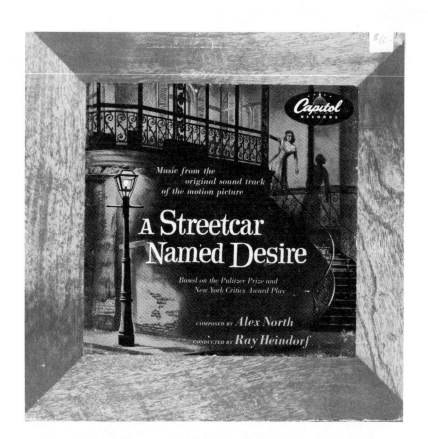

area and develop a sense of the kind of collecting that will please you, you will be in a better position to determine whether and to what extent you want your collection to become specialized.

The Musical Landmarks

The "musical landmarks" are records of sound tracks from movies containing such freshness and verve that they spawned hundreds of imitators, forced a change in the way music was used in movies, had a terrific impact on the musical taste of hundreds of millions of people around the world, and are still magically compelling to new generations years after the sound was first heard. Fifty or more records would fit this definition. Here is a list of ten sound track records that would be the basis of any collection of movie music memorabilia.

1.   Fred Astaire and Ginger Rogers, "Flying Down to Rio" (1933). This was the first film in which Astaire and Rogers were teamed, and the first of a series that made movie musicals an important art and entertainment on a par with theater musicals.

2.   Judy Garland and Mickey Rooney, "Babes in Arms" (1939). This teaming of the two most popular teenagers in the world at the time brought a comic outlook into fashion among youngsters and with it a frantic, dazzling, energetic style that has not been matched since.

3.   The Andrews Sisters in any of their sound tracks beginning with "Argentine Nights." These three dynamos introduced the close harmony singing and adaptation of ethnic melodies from America's big cities which made them a permanent part of movie musical culture.

4.   Bing Crosby, especially his first two movies, "The King of Jazz" (1930), and "The Big Broadcast" (1932). Songs that Crosby made popular, especially during the early years of his movie career, are amazingly evocative of the warm, humorous movies in which he was featured.

5.   Erich Wolfgang Korngold, composer; any sound tracks from movies for which he composed the background music from 1935 to 1941. Some of the original pressings of Korngold's movie music now sell for between $100 and $250 a disk. Korngold was an extremely original European composer who went to Hollywood where he composed operas and concertos and for the musical theater. In addition, he was attracted to the movies where he developed a powerful style for injecting added excitement and pleasure into adventure films that com-

bined romance and derring-do. Korngold composed the music for nearly all of Errol Flynn's costume adventure movies. Among his great recorded scores are "The Adventures of Robin Hood" (1937), and "The Sea Hawk" (1940).

6. Max Steiner, a composer who went to Hollywood from his native Austria on the eve of the first sound movie to begin a career in which he created music for over one hundred major features. It was Steiner who set the standard for bringing together the values of pictures and musical sound; two of his earliest scores are rarities: "Cimarron" (1931), and "The Informer" (1935). He also composed the *Tara* theme from "Gone With the Wind" (1939).

7. Jimmy "Schnozzola" Durante introduced into movie music a highly personal and warmly comical touch with his inimitable "Inka, Dinka Doo," "You Gotta Start Off Each Day with a Smile," and "Umbriago." These songs are on the tracks of many of the films in which he performed during the late 1930s and 1940s, and they all catch his unmistakable qualities.

8. Bernard Herrman, composer of theme music that immediately evokes some of the most important and entertaining dramatic movies ever made: "Citizen Kane" (1941), and most of the Alfred Hitchcock thrillers.

9. Irving Berlin, America's most prolific and best known and loved songwriter. Many Berlin songs were used in movies and on the stage. The track from "Kid Millions" (1934), starring Eddie Cantor, is vital to any collection and a marvelously delightful recording in its own right.

10. Aaron Copland, the dominant serious composer in American life for over forty years, composed music for many movies, and one of his earliest and most memorable was the classic "Of Mice and Men" (1939).

Composers and Songwriters

The list of outstanding composers from all over the world who came to Hollywood in order to try their hand at the great new art form is very long. Some wrote music for only one film and then went home, while others stayed and composed scores and songs for over a hundred movies. In the early days records were not made from the sound tracks and the original playback disk has often either been destroyed, given away, or lost, with the result that little by little, through a combination of restoring a worn sound track enough to make a quality master disk and finding old playbacks, some of the early work of composers for movies is only now beginning to appear. Collectors should seize upon these recordings because they can only increase in value, especially if the sound has been carefully restored. Some European record manufacturers are beginning to specialize in the production of records made from restored old sound tracks using films that were originally distributed for the European market and kept there. The condition of these sound tracks is likely to be better than the frequently adapted versions that circulated in America. Among the composers and lyricists whose names are like gems in the crown of American movie music are: Virgil Thomson, Victor Young, Anton Karas, Jerome Moross, Elmer Bernstein, Miklos Rozsa, Alfred Newman, Dmitri Tiomkin, Ira Gershwin, Sol Kaplan, Jimmy McHugh, Hoagy Carmichael, and Johnny Mercer.

Personalities

Merely the mention of the names of the large number of screen personalities with remarkable voices and performing qualities is enough to evoke much of the joy of the movies of the 1930s. A sampling: Eddie Cantor, Jeannette MacDonald, Gene Autry, Fanny Brice, Deanna Durbin, Betty Grable, Grace Moore, Ezio Pinza, Dinah Shore, Carmen Miranda, Rudy Vallee, and Mae West. These stars and hundreds of others are represented on sound tracks and studio recordings. Generally, the earliest personality records from 1927 to 1930—a short time on the calendar but a very long time in the development of movie sound techniques—are mainly insertions of song and music into a movie. During the first years of sound very little effort was made to develop a musical style that brought out the best in the pictures and which in turn helped to make the music more appealing. As a result, the earliest records are not of great interest to collectors except as curiosities, and this includes the sound track for the first of them—"The Jazz Singer."

Beginning in 1930, movie music made a giant leap and the sound track recordings are gems—and hard to get. The outstanding personality records of the period (sound track only) feature Dick Powell, Maurice Chevalier, Shirley Temple, and Marlene Dietrich. In the last few years, collectors have begun to discover the long neglected and wonderful records of personalities from the late 1930s and early 1940s: Cass Daley, Judy Canova, Lena Horne, Betty Hutton, and Larry Parks.

Themes and Songs

Throughout the world, nearly every regular movie-goer knows and is emotionally moved by the theme music from "Limelight" (Terry's theme), "Gone With the Wind" (Tara's theme), and the hauntingly beautiful love theme from "Dr. Zhivago." Hardly a day goes by in some city of the world when people are not dancing to or singing a theme from a movie—activities that are even more popular nowadays than they were during the early days of sound movies. Among the notable themes that would form part of any collection are recordings of the theme music from the Laurel and Hardy movies, the Terry Toon music, "The Third Man," "High Noon," and the 1943 classic "Casablanca."

Individual songs, in studio or sound track versions, that are among the most in demand by collectors are not necessarily from the all-time favorite movies, from Academy Award winning pictures, or even from movies that are well remembered or shown from time to time on television. These are songs that evoke the movies in which they appeared but are better remembered than the movies, even though they are movie songs through and through. Among them are such outstanding movie songs as: "Blue Skies," "Happy Days Are Here Again," "All of Me," "Jeannine," "Minnie the Moocher," "I Feel a Song Coming On," and "Boulevard of Broken Dreams."

Entire Films

For most collectors one of the most satisfying leisure time activities and most profitable sides of record collecting is in connection with well-edited musical portions of the sound tracks of entire movie musicals. These are very scarce and very valuable. Probably no more than about sixty sound track recordings of the great musical movies from 1927 to 1941 were made and edited. The recordings made after 1941 are generally of good quality, carefully edited, and still available at reasonable prices. Because the later discs were made by the hundreds of thousands and because they are still available to new collectors through new releases or the originals, the price has gone up only slightly. The pre-1941 full sound track records, however, were made in very small quantities—as there was little demand at the time—and the cost has gone up steeply. Some of the most important movie music recordings include sound track versions from the following fabulous movies: "Broadway Melody," "The Desert Song," "King of Jazz," "Gold Diggers of Broadway," "Whoopee," "Footlight Parade," "Forty-Second Street," "Love Me Tonight," "The Great Ziegfeld," "The Wizard of Oz," "Strike Up the Band," "For Me and My Gal," "Alice in Wonderland," "An American in Paris," "Merry Widow," "Annie Get Your Gun," "With a Song in My Heart," and "Because You're Mine."

Some Collecting Tips

Record jackets, with and without movie themes, came into use only after the mid-1940s; the early 78rpms were sold either in individual dust protectors that contained no artwork, or, if there were two or more records in a set, in a plain album. The earliest movie music records also had, on occasion, interesting labels, not from a design standpoint but because of the valuable information furnished on the label about the movie, the performers and musicians, and the year of manufacture. When buying, be careful not to pay for the record jacket artwork alone; make your final decision only after hearing the entire record.

With the growing interest in movie memorabilia, movie companies are making records, from the original playback disks or sound tracks, of many all-time favorites. Such items as the records for "That's Entertainment" and "That's Entertainment II," along with records of sound tracks for many old Warner Brothers classics, are bound to become valuable collector's items in the years ahead.

Current Prices for First Release, Original Pressing of Sound Tracks

Records are in good to excellent condition, from a sound-quality standpoint, and probably used.

Film	Key Point of Interest	Price
Alias Jimmy Valentine	song "Love Dreams." Among first features movies to use a song	$175.00
Alice in Wonderland	marvelously nostalgic singing by the great comic Ed Wynn	50.00
An American in Paris	many songs by Ira and George Gershwin	60.00
Animal Crackers	song "Hooray for Capt. Spalding" and classic wit by the Marx Brothers	200.00

Film	Key Point of Interest	Price
Awakening	"Marie"—one of the most widely known songs of all time	250.00
The Band Wagon	delightful singing by Fred Astaire from the repertoire of the Howard Dietz and Arthur Schwartz team	25.00
Blessed Event	debut singing by Dick Powell	225.00
The Blue Angel	Marlene Dietrich's 1930 film-music great "Falling in Love Again"	300.00
Bright Eyes	debut singing by Jane Withers	125.00
Chasing Rainbows	first appearance of the song that has become the theme song of all political parties: "Happy Days Are Here Again"	150.00
Dancing Lady	debut appearance of Fred Astaire	320.00
Divine Lady	one of the first songs to be featured in a dramatic movie: "Lady Divine"	200.00
Every Night at Eight	debut singing by Frances Langford	175.00
The Fleet's In	debut singing by Betty Hutton	250.00
Good News	striking harmonies by June Allyson and Peter Lawford	60.00
The Great Victor Herbert	debut singing by Mary Martin	125.00
The Great Ziegfeld	debut of Ray Bolger	250.00
Follow Through	movie version of the famed Broadway song "Button Up Your Overcoat"	75.00
For Me and My Gal	among the first features to use a specially composed song	125.00
I Dream of Lilac Time	the origin of the immortal song "Jeannine"	250.00
Jungle Princess	debut of Dorothy Lamour	110.00
Kid Boots	singing debut of the incomparable Eddie Cantor	300.00
The Last Time I Saw Paris	the origin of the unbeatable song "Lady Be Good"	75.00

Film	Key Point of Interest	Price
Love Me or Leave Me	fresh harmonies by James Cagney and Doris Day	30.00
The Love Parade	singing debut of Jeannette MacDonald	500.00
Merry Widow	a collector's favorite with early singing by Lana Turner	100.00
Oceana Roll	a rediscovered gem featuring the Andrews Sisters	40.00
On With the Show	one of the firsts (1929) of famed Ethel Waters	350.00
Pinocchio	a beautiful version of "When You Wish Upon a Star"	35.00
Red Haired Alibi	debut of Shirley Temple	500.00
Rhythm on the Range	debut of Martha Raye	300.00
Roadhouse Nights	debut of Jimmy Durante	375.00
Roman Scandals	debut of Lucille Ball	225.00
A Streetcar Named Desire	remarkable score for an important Brando movie	60.00
Serenade	among the best and most complete examples of Mario Lanza's singing	10.00
Show Boat	Kathryn Grayson at her best	85.00
Three Smart Girls	debut of Deanna Durbin	150.00
Up in Arms	the fabulous Danny Kaye in his debut film performance	275.00
The Vagabond Lover	debut of Rudy Vallee	250.00
Zorba the Greek	the first American film featuring a score by the famed Greek composer Mikis Theodorakis	10.00

CHAPTER NINE

Archives, Special Collectors and Collections, Museums, Libraries, Shows

I recently made a sentimental pilgrimage to a neighborhood where I had lived with my family for a few years in the 1930s. I recalled from my childhood that there were several movie houses in the neighborhood and as I strolled I looked for them. One of them, the largest, had been torn down to make way for a deep automobile expressway that cut through the heart of the neighborhood; a second was converted to a massive horse betting parlor; a third, one that for some reason I had rarely gone to, was being used exclusively for science-fiction and horror movies; a fourth, a place I remember going frequently with my mother on Wednesday nights so that we could both go home with a new addition to my mother's collection of movie-theme dinner plates, had become specialized in showing only Kung Fu (the oriental martial art) movies. I searched for a long time for the movie house where, on Saturdays during my childhood, a ten-cent admission would provide a bag of candy, from one-cent to five-cent surprises in the candy package, an adventure serial, six or more short cartoons including at least one "Popeye," and two and sometimes three features. We lined up at ten in the morning and got out at around three with plenty of time left for outdoor play. There were retail shops in the area where the movie house had been and it was only when I noticed the entrance to a large shoe store paved in the colors and terrazzo design of the old movie houses that I felt I had found an unmistakable sign of my favorite—the *Plaza*.

Tracking down sources of interesting or rare movie memorabilia— that is, sources that you believe have not been tapped before—will be a fun-filled adventure and well worth undertaking. As you stroll about,

Windows of Cinemabilia, New York.   *Photo by Dan Asher.*

looking and thinking about unusual places for "prospecting," you will probably have occasion to understand, more than once, why movie memorabilia are able to stir up such strong and good feelings.

Prospecting has a double value. First, you will from time to time come upon some real treasures of movie material. Second, prospecting will lead you to some important collections of materials where you will be able to see the results of major collecting activities and develop a sense of the value attached to the materials by other collectors.

Nearly every college library and many public libraries are developing collections of movie materials containing books about movies, novelizations, sound tracks, posters, and a host of other items. Most libraries in this country will probably soon have permanent collections of movie memorabilia to view, take home on loan, and enjoy. Even now, as the libraries strive to develop collections by making purchases from dealers and dealer-collectors, they are places where you can become familiar with some of the many different examples of memorabilia. Not many local libraries are going to be able to exhibit the treasures that the Smithsonian Institution in Washington, D.C., has collected but they will, on a smaller scale, resemble the Smithsonian collection since they will have to acquire materials from a large number of private collectors in order to obtain variety and high quality.

Performing arts centers have sprung up around the country in recent years and are also slowly developing collections of movie memorabilia. They may serve the collector as places to view different types of collections, and as prospective purchasers of unusual memorabilia and often entire collections.

Libraries, performing arts centers, and museums are also likely to be helpful to collectors because they employ specialized research librarians who, even when they are not collectors themselves, are unusually qualified and knowledgeable about where and how to learn more about particular items or categories of memorabilia. Librarians or archivists of special collections in museums and universities will be especially helpful in providing you with information about a particular period in movie making and often about specific connections between a kind of memorabilia and the personality or movie that inspired it.

The nation's oldest and most complete movie archive is the film department of the Museum of Modern Art in New York City. The film department was started in 1935 and its archives include 8000 movies, 2000 scripts, 3000 movie posters, numerous original sketches for movie

Interior of Cinemabilia, New York.   *Photo by Dan Asher.*

Interior of Cinemabilia, New York.   *Photo by Dan Asher.*

sets and costumes, original music scores, and tens of thousands of clippings, books, and other documents. The film center exhibits films to over 300,000 people a year, runs a circulating collection, and provides resources for research. These resources are indispensable for people writing on the movies or building up private collections. From time to time the Museum organizes shows of materials from its movie archives and publishes a catalogue of the items exhibited. These catalogues are very valuable items in themselves to some collectors and are unusually useful sources of information.

By far the most complete archive of movie materials and most unique collection of its type in the world is the Theatre Collection of the New York City Public Library. Located among the buildings that make up the Lincoln Center for the Performing Arts complex in New York, the Theatre Collection has built up a monumental collection of nearly every kind of *paper* memorabilia that has ever been produced in any language. There are well preserved photographs, prints, posters, programs, original drawings for sets, costumes and props, caricatures of thousands of film performers and other personalities, clippings, and letters, along with several million stills. The library archive contains movie materials that go back to 1907 and its collection of fan magazines is the largest in the world. However, much of it has been vandalized, with the result that the library is beginning to allow people to see these materials only as microfilm reproductions.

Starting in 1928, the Association of Movie Producers and Distributors began to make an annual gift to the Library of materials produced by the movie industry (other than films) so that the Library could store, classify, preserve, and make the materials available to researchers and collectors. In the Library you will be able to see and touch the many precious scrapbooks about movies prepared by the stars themselves, such as those of Lillian and Dorothy Gish and Richard Barthelmess. The archive contains individual file folders for thousands of actors, actresses, and directors, along with composers and producers. These precious files were built up by gifts of material and regular mailings from the publicity departments of the studios, as well as material purchased by the library from private collectors. Many collectors and dealers who are not able to use the resources of the archive personally find it helpful to write or telephone the extremely talented and helpful research librarians of the archive to get their questions answered. When I use the archive I am always impressed that hardly an hour goes by without a telephone call from a movie memorabilia collector or dealer from some distant point in the United States asking for specific information about a performer or a movie, or for an important bit of background information about either.

Many of the major movie production companies, such as Paramount, Twentieth Century-Fox, United Artists, Warner Brothers, and M-G-M no longer have the complete archives they maintained until the 1950s but have started to re-build their collections on a highly selective basis and have turned to private collectors to provide materials. They do maintain libraries and modest research departments and will be helpful in answering specific questions about personalities who worked for them, or about their movies and other materials. Many large advertising, public relations, and publicity companies that developed movie promotion materials over the years have archives and libraries where they preserve memorabilia, and they occasionally sell objects to collectors. Restricted sale to discerning collectors is also practiced by certain large printing companies and distributors who have maintained substantial archives of movie materials going back fifty years. Also, some large record companies which made records from sound tracks as well as sheet music companies keep up good archives and research libraries which they allow collectors to use upon written request, and they are known to sell items for specialized collections on occasion.

You can easily imagine that the most fabulous collections of movie memorabilia, although not by any means the most comprehensive, are to be found in California—the state that nurtured the movie industry. There are dozens of public and private collections of movie materials in Hollywood alone which are open to the public, and there are several major dealers who receive requests from dealers and collectors all over the world. Among the great public collections is that of the Los Angeles County Museum of History and Science. The Museum has one of the largest and finest collections of scripts, costumes, posters, props, and autographed portraits to be found anywhere in the world, and much of the collection represents gifts of personal materials from many famous stars such as Charlie Chaplin, Douglas Fairbanks, Lon Chaney, and Marie Dressler.

The Los Angeles Theatre Arts Library contains the personal production notebooks and marked screenplay scripts of numerous directors. It also has set sketches and exciting story boards which show the artistic development of scenes. The library also houses all of the movie materials produced by and for the famed Keystone Production Company as well as almost all of the press books produced by Universal Pictures. The movie archive of the University of Southern California at University Park in Los Angeles is the custodian of the remarkable collections of Cecil B. DeMille; the collection includes the film research library that Paramount once used and the early materials of the Hal Roach studios. Since none of these archives and special collections are *complete* collections, the curators are constantly seeking out private collectors and dealers who have materials that can be added to the collections.

Among the remarkable movie memorabilia collections that may be viewed by the public is that of Mrs. T. Yeandle, who made a gift of 91 scrapbooks to Dartmouth College in Hanover, New Hampshire. The collection was compiled between 1920 and 1950 and contains stills from nearly all of the feature movies shown in America during those years. The most abundant archive of all is that of the United States Library of Congress, but its collection may only be used for study purposes and it is rare for exhibitions to be arranged for the public. This treasure trove includes the bulk of the private collection of materials compiled by Mary Pickford; the collection of George Kleine, containing tens of thousands of clippings about the movies from 1910 on; there are also 75,000 reels of movies from the world over, including 3000 reels of movies made before 1910. The Library of Congress also owns an extraordinary collection of movie posters, stills, costumes, and other precious memorabilia.

Although there are hundreds of movie memorabilia dealers throughout the United States (and a growing number in other countries), there are two that deserve special mention. One is *Larry Edmond's Bookshop* in Hollywood, the other is *Cinemabilia* in New York City.

Cinemabilia and *Larry Edmond's Bookshop* are in many ways a combination of archive, research library, superstore of memorabilia, and art gallery. Both shops are superbly up-to-date in terms of being able to have available the kinds of memorabilia that most collectors, established as well as beginning, want to own as well as a surprising amount of high quality materials which appeals to highly specialized collectors. The proprietors and staff in both shops are extremely knowledgeable and helpful in aiding collectors to ferret out exactly the kinds of material they want for their collections. They also buy individual items and entire collections and pay premium prices. Both dealers have a reasonable research service available for collectors who want to acquire authentic hard-to-find or rare memorabilia. The Hollywood shop is more specialized in books about the movies and the New York City shop is more specialized in movie graphics. Many dealers around the country at one time worked for either shop or made their first purchases for their collections at these places. Both shops will make exchanges to assist collectors and collector-dealers and will accept items for sale from collectors on a consignment basis. They both have carefully prepared catalogues of their materials and are extremely reliable in conducting transactions by mail order. Both shops set a high standard of excellence, and as many more collectors become dealers they will have a good example to follow.

In addition to movie memorabilia dealers, there are hundreds of collector-dealers who have amassed extraordinary collections of specialized materials and who operate modest businesses, usually from their homes, selling materials from their collections. One of the leading collector-dealers is Gene Andrewski. Gene was raised in a small Oklahoma town and used to race down to Main Street early in the morning on the days that the movie house was about to change its programs. In this way, he was able to collect hundreds of stills, lobby cards, inserts, posters, and other promotional materials. Over the years, Gene collected nearly a million items that form a rare archive. He is one of the leading collectors of materials on female stars and book writers, and television producers and show organizers often turn to him both for advice and for the use of his collection for their own projects. He is well informed and extremely helpful to beginning collectors, taking time to explain the whys and hows of successful collecting. Gene also maintains a catalog of some of his collection for mail order business.

Another private collector-dealer, now living in New York City but originally from Oakland, California, is Alan Barbour. Alan is author of a number of movie books and is the leading collector of memorabilia about serials and "B" Westerns. You have only to mention a fragment of a scene from a serial made in 1934, for example, and within a few minutes Alan will tell you who acted in the film, the name of the movie and its director, and which studio produced it; and while telling you all this he will come up with a black-and-white still of exactly the scene you described and a collection of the ads that were used to promote the serial! He's phenomenal and has a phenomenal collection. Alan also travels a great deal to speak at shows and symposia. He keeps an up-to-date catalogue of his collection and conducts an efficient, high-quality mail order business.

Both Gene Andrewski and Alan Barbour are involved in another aspect of movie memorabilia—the development of future collectors' items. Therefore, in addition to his many other activities, Gene designs movie games that are informative, entertaining, and provide copies of actual movie materials as part of the game. A Movie Monster board game, invented by Gene, introduces the players to an extremely popular area for collecting. Alan Barbour produces special magazines that feature the personalities and scenes from "B" Westerns and serials. In time, the games and the magazines will themselves become items for memorabilia collectors.

Since the mid-1960s, movie memorabilia shows have become increasingly popular. Some of the shows are part of other organized promotions such as Nostalgia Shows, Comics Conventions, Antiques Exhibits, Americana Fairs, Crafts Fairs, and so forth, but more and more movie memorabilia shows are being run on an exclusive basis. In 1976, for example, the Bijou Society, an organization of movie collectors that was set up in 1975, ran a national Movie Memorabilia Show in Hollywood which was attended by over 5000 people. The annual "B" Western Convention, held every year since 1968 in Nashville, began with about 300 participants, and had over 4500 participants in 1976. The memorabilia conventions are worth attending because they bring together virtually every kind of collection in one place for you to see, touch, and compare prices. Generally, dealers and collector-dealers rent space to exhibit and sell on a daily basis or during the entire period of the convention, which usually lasts about three days. There are two to three important shows being run somewhere every month of the year, and since the almost permanent "flea markets" are beginning to have more movie materials than they did about ten years ago, you can enjoy a wide selection of places to search for materials worth collecting.

Guide to Dealers and Collector–Dealers

Key:	B&W	= Black-and-white stills
	C	= Catalog is available
	Co	= Color
	F	= Fan magazines
	G	= General collection
	I	= Inquire for requests
	M	= Sheet music
	MO	= Mail Order
	P	= Posters

Pa   = Paper, small objects like Big Little Books
S   = Scripts
ST   = Sound Tracks
3-D = Decorative memorabilia, curios, knicknacks

ABACUS HOBBIES
218 NE First Avenue
Miami, Florida

G   MO   C

ACE BOOK STORE
5400 Euclid Avenue
Cleveland, Ohio

G   MO   C

AFTER THE CHASE
Lison, Ohio

3-D   I

ALDREDGE BOOK STORE
2506 Cedar Springs
Dallas, Texas

G   MO   I

ALLEN, JOHN E.
92 Highland Street
Park Ridge, New Jersey

G   MO   C

ANDREWSKI, GENE
165 West 91st Street
New York, New York

B&W   MO   C   I

**ANG & LIL'S COLLECTOR'S
CORNER**
24 Bennington Drive
Rochester, New York

G   MO   I

B. BOB'S ANTIQUES
136-38 38th Avenue
Flushing, New York

3-D   MO   I

BACKYARD ANTIQUES
71 Merritt Avenue
Dumont, New Jersey

3-D   MO   I

BARBOUR, ALAN
P.O. Box 154
Kew Gardens, New York

B&W   P   G   MO   C   I

BIJOU SOCIETY
7800 Conser Place
Shawnee Mission, Kansas

G   MO   C   I

BRANDT, EDDY
Memory Shop
Hollywood, California

G   MO   C   I

**BRUNSVOLD'S CINEMA
BOOK SERVICE**
244 West Beech Street
San Diego, California

G   MO   C   I

Larry Edmonds Bookshop, Hollywood, California—a major center for West Coast collectors.

CARRINGTON, JOHN
654 A Ramblewood Lane
Freemansburg, Pennsylvania

P 3-D MO C I

CASANOVA, JACK
1623 West Greenfield Avenue
Milwaukee, Wisconsin

G MO I

CHEROKEE BOOK SHOP
6638 Hollywood Boulevard
Hollywood, California

G MO C I

CINEMA ATTIC
Department MT, P.O. Box 7772
Philadelphia, Pennsylvania

G MO C I

CINEMABILIA
10 West 13th Street
New York, New York

G P MO C I

COLLECTOR'S BOOKSTORE
6763 Hollywood Boulevard
Hollywood, California

G MO C I

COLLECTOR'S SHOP
5720 2nd Street
South Arlington, Virginia

G MO C I

CUDAHY NEWS &
  HOBBY SHOP
4727 South Packard Avenue
Milwaukee, Wisconsin

G MO I

DALLAS LITERARY SHOP
4934 Maple Avenue
Dallas, Texas

G MO I

DARROW'S, CHICK
Fun Antiques
1174 Second Avenue
New York, New York

3-D MO I

DEARDON, W. ROWLAND
221 Rodman Avenue
Jenkintown, Pennsylvania

G MO I

DEL'S BOOK SERVICE
12725 Flatbush Avenue
Norwalk, Connecticut

G MO I

DOWN MEMORY LANE
1108 West Main Street
Oklahoma City, Oklahoma

G MO I

EASON PUBLICATIONS
1289 Beach Valley Road, N.E.
Atlanta, Georgia

B&W MO I

EDMUND'S, LARRY
Book Shop
6658 Hollywood Boulevard
Hollywood, California

G   MO   C   I

EDWARDS, FRANCES
647 Main Street
Hartford, Connecticut

G   MO   I

FANTASY SHOP
1053 South Clinton Avenue
Rochester, New York

G   MO   I

FOUST, LEE
66 Alberta Terrace
Walnut Creek, California

G   MO   I

FREESON, LEE
P.O. Box 922
Hollywood, California

G   MO   I

GALLAGHER, PAUL J.
234 Jerome Street
Brooklyn, New York

Pa   MO   I

GLOVER, THOMAS L.
320 Atlantic Avenue
Trenton, New Jersey

G   MO   I

HAKE, TED & JONELL
1753 Westwood Road
York, Pennsylvania

3-D   MO   C   I

HAMPTON BOOKS
Box 76
Newberry, South Carolina

G   MO   I

HECHT, P. M.
383 East 17th Street
Brooklyn, New York

3-D   MO   I

HERITAGE RECORDING
   SERVICE
340 Parker Street
Newton Centre, Massachusetts

ST   MO   C   I

HOBBYVILLE
440 West 34th Street
New York, New York

B&W   MO   C   I

HOFFMAN, PAM & JERRY
Duncanville Bookstore
106 West Camp Wisdom Road
Duncanville, Texas

G   MO   C   I

HOUSE OF BROWSE
13151 West Dixie Highway
North Miami, Florida

G   MO   I

HOUSE OF OLDIES
267 Bleecker Street
New York, New York

ST   MO   I

HUNT, JACK
2811 Delaware Avenue, Kenmore
Buffalo, New York

G   MO   I

JACOBOWITZ, BILL
436 Lincoln Avenue
Orange, New Jersey

Pa   MO   I

JAY BEE MAGAZINES
776 Eighth Avenue
New York, New York

B&W   MO   I

JON'S WORLD
Village of Old Forge
Morristown, New Jersey

G   MO   I

JOYCE BOOKSHOP
1116 Franklin
Oakland, California

G   MO   I

KELLEHER, WILLIAM F.
544 Westview Avenue
Cliffside Park, New Jersey

G   MO   I

KONJURA, EDWARD
6488 Fenhurst Avenue
Parma Heights, Ohio

G   MO   I

KULIK, TODD
81 Christie Avenue
Clifton, New Jersey

G   MO   I

LA BRIOLA, RAY
72-31 150th Street
Flushing, New York

3-D   MO   I

LANGLEY ASSOCIATES
5728 Shaefer
Dearborn, Michigan

B&W   P   Co   MO   C

LEVINE, ALAN
P.O. Box 1577
Bloomfield, New Jersey

P   MO   I

MANESIS, DALE
The Good Old Days
960 North 27th Street
Milwaukee, Wisconsin

G   MO   I

MANKETO'S MEMORABILIA
  SHOPS
270 Fulton Avenue
Hempstead, New York

G   MO   I

MARY'S MEMORIES
P.O. Box 222
Glendale, California

G   M   MO   I

MEMORY SHOP
109 East 12th Street
New York, New York

B&W   Co   MO   I

MOVIE MEMORABILIA SHOP
   OF HOLLYWOOD
P.O. Box 29027
Los Angeles, California

G   F   MO   I

MOVIE STAR NEWS
212 East 14th Street
New York, New York

B&W   MO   I

N. E. MERCANTILE CO.
1204 N. Lamar Boulevard
Austin, Texas

G

NICOLA BOOK STORE
13 East Lake Street
Minneapolis, Minnesota

G   MO   I

NOSTALGIA ENTERPRISES
11702 Venice Boulevard
Los Angeles, California

G   MO   I

NOSTALGIA SHOP
3905 West Lawrence Avenue
Chicago, Illinois

G   MO   I

OHLINGER, JERRY
101 West 78th Street
New York, New York

B&W   P   S   MO   C

OLD NEW YORK
   BOOK SHOP
1453 Piedmont Road, N.E.
Atlanta, Georgia

G   MO   I

PASSAIC BOOK CENTER
594 Main Avenue
Passaic, New Jersey

G   MO   I

PENNY ARCADE
1164 Second Avenue
New York, New York

3-D   Pa   MO   I

PICKWICK BOOKSHOP
6743 Hollywood Boulevard
Hollywood, California

G   MO   I

PIN ON
645 West End Avenue
New York, New York

3-D   MO   I

PLAZA BOOK SHOP
380 Broadway
Albany, New York

G MO I

PREMIUM PRODUCTS
339 West 44th Street
New York, New York

B&W P MO I

REID, THOMAS
35 Mertz Avenue
Belleville, New Jersey

Pa MO I

ROGERS, TOM
601 East 80th Street
Brooklyn, New York

G MO I

ROGOFSKY, HOWARD
Box CJ 1102
Flushing, New York

G MO C I

ROMAINE, PAUL
192 N. Clark Street
Chicago, Illinois

G MO I

ROY BANARRIO
Roy's Memory Shop
Houston, Texas

G MO I

S & S ANTIQUES
P.O. Box 831
Union, New Jersey

3-D MO I

SANDAGURSKY'S HAPPY
 DAYS
15 Hawthorne Court
Centerport, New York

G MO I

SARYIAN, PAUL
Nostalgia
P.O. Box 265
Staten Island, New York

G MO I

SCHULTZ, KENNETH C.
Box M 753
Hoboken, New Jersey

3-D MO I

SEULING, PHIL
Box 177
Coney Island Station
Brooklyn, New York

G MO C I

SHUTE, CLARK A.
132 Lawnwood Avenue
Longmeadow, Massachusetts

G MO I

SILVER SCREEN
1192 Lexington Avenue
New York, New York

G MO C I

SMITH, PACKY
P.O. Box 17059
Nashville, Tennessee

G   MO   I

TANNER, MILES
Ft. Worth, Texas

G   MO   I

TOM'S NOSTALGIA SHOP
5124 South Kedzie
Chicago, Illinois

G   MO   I

VESPER, A. F.
RFD 1
Suncock, New Hampshire

G   MO   I

WINDSOR GALLERIES
1013 North Charles St.
Baltimore, Maryland

G   MO   I

YESTERDAY
174-A Ninth Avenue
New York, New York

P   MO   C   I

YESTERDAY BOOKS
1631 West Wells
Milwaukee, Wisconsin

G   MO   I

Index

173